American Synagogues

# American Synagogues

## A Century of Architecture and Jewish Community

Samuel D. Gruber
Photography by Paul Rocheleau
Edited by Scott J. Tilden

For Judy, Jonah, and Zoë

The photographer wishes to thank Elaine Rocheleau and Raymond Alvarez.

Rizzoli editor: Ellen R. Cohen
Copyeditor: Elizabeth Johnson
Design by Binocular, New York

First published in the United States of America in 2003
by Rizzoli International Publications, Inc.
300 Park Avenue South
New York, NY 10010
www.rizzoliusa.com



2003 2004 2005 2006 2007 / 10 9 8 7 6 5 4 3 2 1

Printed in China

ISBN: 0-8478-2549-3

Library of Congress Catalog Control Number: 2003104756

# Contents

# List of Synagogues

# Acknowledgments

Samuel D. Gruber

I would like to thank Scott Tilden and Paul Rocheleau for inviting me to join them in this book project, and Carol Herselle Krinsky for suggesting me to them. It has been a happy collaboration, and I thank Scott for his many questions and insights, and Paul for his keen eye, superb grasp of the essence of architecture, and on-site ingenuity.

For over a decade, Carol Krinsky has been a teacher and guide for me, opening the world of synagogue architecture. Besides her authoritative book on the Synagogues of Europe, which continues to be a wellspring of information, it was a short article by Carol about Norman Jaffe's Gates of Grove Synagogue in East Hampton that showed me that there were other fine modern synagogues besides the oft-illustrated Beth Sholom by Frank Lloyd Wright. Since that time I have lamented the lack of information on these, and so am especially glad to write this book. I would also like to thank Ken Frieden at Syracuse University who encouraged me to teach a course on the American synagogue, and to my students who helped me explore the subject.

This book would not have been possible without the unfailing cooperation of dozens of synagogue administrators, rabbis, librarians, receptionists, and custodians. The custodians especially deserve recognition—they are the ones who were always there to open the doors, adjust the lights, and generally help out with our photo shoots. Amazingly, even in the aftermath of the September 11th attacks, only one synagogue refused to allow photographs of its facilities.

I would like to thank the librarians at Syracuse University, especially Barbara Opar and Randy Bond, as well as the interlibrary loan office. In addition, the Asher Library of the Spertus Institute of Jewish Studies in Chicago, the Avery Architecture Library at Columbia University in New York, the Fine Arts Department of the Boston Public Library, the International Survey of Jewish Monuments, and the Ricker Library at the University of Illinois in Urbana all supplied special materials. My colleagues on the Society of Architectural Historians listserve have also been ready with information about worthy, but sometimes obscure architects.

Thank you also to Rabbi Daniel Freelander of the Union of American Hebrew Congregations, and to my friends Marilyn Chiat, Esther Goldman, and David Kaufman for their advice. Special thanks to my own rabbi, Sheldon Ezring of Temple Society of Concord in Syracuse, and to temple Administrator Howard Brodsky, who have allowed me to see the everyday working of a synagogue close-up. This book is also better through the kind participation of many architects including Jay Brown, Will Bruder, Alex Gorlin, Eddie Jacobs, and Michael Laudau, who generously shared information and ideas about their buildings, and the artist Louis Kaish who kindly spent a day with me discussing her life and art. Thanks also to my friends at the School of Architecture at Syracuse University who listened to my ideas.

Thanks to the book's production and editorial team, Ellen Cohen and Elizabeth Johnson. Thanks to Charles Miers at Universe who quickly showed interest in this project, and thanks to our agent, Sheryl Shade of Shade Global who turned interest into substance.

Lastly, I want to thank my family, to whom this book is dedicated, for their support. I especially commend my nine-year old daughter Zoë who was willing to trudge through the rain with me to visit the Hevra of the Southern Berkshires, while her mother and brother oversaw the car repairs at a garage in Great Barrington.

Opposite: Temple Beth Sholom, Miami Beach, Florida. Detail of the patterned stained-glass windows in the sanctuary.

# Preface

Scott J. Tilden



> One thing have I desired of the LORD, that will I seek after; that I may dwell in the house of the LORD all the days of my life, to behold the beauty of the LORD, and to enquire in his temple.
>
> —Psalms 27

When I was living in Chicago, my brother urged me to make an architectural pilgrimage to North Shore Congregation Israel synagogue in Glencoe, Illinois. When I walked into the sanctuary, I was struck dumb by the majesty of the space and the play of light on the golden Ark, the container of the sacred Torah. The architect of this exquisite structure was Minoru Yamasaki, the designer of the World Trade Center in New York City.

Twenty years later, while reading a book on Frank Lloyd Wright, I saw a photograph of his synagogue Beth Shalom in Elkins Park, Pennsylvania. Again impressed by the beauty and originality of the design, I began conducting research and discovered that many of the greatest architects of the twentieth century designed American synagogues. In addition to Wright and Yamasaki, the list included Walter Gropius, Eric Mendelsohn, Albert Kahn, Pietro Belluschi, Marcel Breuer, Philip Johnson, Robert A.M. Stern, Paul Rudolph, and Louis Kahn. Yet I learned from talking with friends and architectural colleagues that most were unaware of this outstanding architectural legacy. They suggested I develop an illustrated book on these modern American synagogues, because no book in print focused exclusively on this distinguished group of buildings.

Carol Herselle Krinsky of the NYU Art History Department provided valuable advice on this book project, including her suggestion for the ideal author, Samuel Gruber. He received his M.A., M.Phil., and Ph.D. degrees from Columbia University in the History of Art and Archaeology. He is Director of the Jewish Heritage Research Center, Research Director of the U.S. Commission for the Preservation of America's Heritage Abroad (USCPAHA), and serves as consultant to the Jewish Heritage Program of the World Monuments Fund (WMF).

Sam and I shared the same vision for the book. It would explore exceptional works of architecture of American synagogues from 1900 to the present. But the book would not simply be an architectural history. It would also be a social history of American Jews as revealed in synagogue architecture. The book would examine the movement of many American Jews to the suburbs and the very different designs of urban and suburban synagogues. The book would document how the changing role of women and evolving liturgical practices shaped the plans of these structures. Sam also wished to highlight the designs of contemporary architects. He selected synagogues to include in the book by Norman Jaffe, Alexander Gorlin, Lake/Flato, Will Bruder, Louis Goodman, Michael Landau, and Levin/Brown & Associates.

I had only one choice for photographer, Paul Rocheleau. I worked successfully with Paul on the recently published architectural monograph *Daniel H. Burnham*. I admired his beautiful images in earlier books on Frank Lloyd Wright, Henry Hobson Richardson, and Frederick Law Olmsted. By using a single photographer with a single perspective, this book reveals a whole constellation of buildings, which can be compared to one another to measure consistency and contradiction of design and decoration.

Sam, Paul, and I worked together for over a year on creating this book. Our collective journey revealed an abundance of beautiful synagogues by famous architects and notable designers largely unknown today. Our difficulty was in selecting approximately thirty synagogues that represented the full range of designs of the past century.

I want to thank Sam and Paul for their exceptional efforts in creating this book. Charles Miers of Universe and Rizzoli made this project possible and enjoyable through his unflagging support. The rabbis and administrators at the various synagogues generously provided historic materials to Sam and facilitated Paul's photographic work. Sam, Paul, and I hope that through our efforts the noteworthy architecture of American synagogues becomes better known and appreciated.

Opposite: North Shore Congregation Israel, Glencoe, Illinois. The ground level windows connect the sanctuary to the beautiful natural setting of the synagogue, on the shores of Lake Michigan.

# Introduction

And they said: Let us arise and build. So they strengthened their hands for the good work.

—Nehamiah 2:17–18

The twentieth century was a remarkable period for the growth and acceptance of Judaism in the United States. The American Jewish population rose from a few hundred thousand people, settled mostly in Eastern cities, to a population of more than five million spread across every state. The century saw massive immigration in its early years, followed by an anti-Semitic backlash in many segments of society. Despite this, Judaism emerged as a recognized religion on near-equal footing with the established Protestant and Catholic churches, so much so that by mid-century the religious configuration of the nation was regularly defined by the three faiths. The second half of the century witnessed the rapid demolition of many social, economic, and political barriers that kept Jewish Americans from full participation in secular society. As acceptance increased so did assimilation, until Jews and Jewish culture were firmly embedded in the American mainstream.

Throughout this period the erection of synagogues played a significant role in defining Jewish identity and conveying Jewish values and aspirations to the non-Jewish American majority. The design and building of synagogues helped chart a course for Jewish communal and religious life in a democratic, pluralistic society. Just as often, synagogues sought to adapt their mission and their forms to better reflect and serve the Jewish population's changing attitudes and behavior, over which organized religion seemed to have little control. During this process major social upheaval, including the Great Depression, World War II, the Holocaust, and the civil rights movement, all had tremendous influence on the development of American Jewish identity and the role of Jews in American life.

This book traces the development of one building type over one tumultuous century—the synagogue. But even in a book devoted to this one subject, not all the factors affecting synagogue design and evolution, use and perception, can be fully addressed. Additionally, only a small fraction of the thousands of synagogues erected in this country can be mentioned, let alone discussed. However, the sample of synagogues chosen for representation in this book has been carefully considered to represent the range of synagogue design over the span of one hundred years and much of the best work done by master architects.

For nearly 250 years, Jewish communities in the United States have been erecting synagogues, and from the first, these buildings have been the preeminent visible symbols of Judaism in the New World. Over time, synagogues have also become the central focus of American Jewish identity even at a time when the majority of American Jews do not attend regularly synagogue services or other synagogue events.

The oldest surviving synagogue in the United States is the Touro Synagogue, an outstanding work of colonial architecture designed by prominent architect Peter Harrison and completed in 1763.[1] The erection of Touro Synagogue began a tradition in which leading architects—first non-Jewish and later, as the profession changed, including Jewish architects—gave their talents to the creation of Jewish houses of worship. Looking back over two and a half centuries, the list of notable architects who have designed synagogues is indeed impressive: Peter Harrison; William Strickland; Thomas U. Walter; John MacCarthur; Leopold Eidlitz; Henry Fernbach; Frank Furness; Dankmar Adler and Louis Sullivan; Arnold Brunner; Henry Hornbostel; Albert Kahn; William Tachau; Alfred Alschuler; Eric Mendelsohn; Percival Goodman; Frank Lloyd Wright; Walter Gropius; Minoru Yamasaki; Philip Johnson; Louis Kahn; Werner Seligmann; Pietro Belluschi; Harrison & Abramovitz; Paul Rudolph; Marcel Breuer; David, Brody & Associates; and many others.

The buildings of these masters vary dramatically. Occasionally, the differences are so extreme that were it not for the similarity of function, it might be difficult to group these structures together as a single building type. Yet, despite formal and stylistic variations in materials, elements, and decorations, the overriding similarities of function unite these buildings. There is constancy among them to be discovered, but also an evolution of function and form to be traced—one that parallels changes within American Judaism, and occasionally anticipates them.

This book goes to great lengths to show many views of each synagogue, especially of the interiors. Every building needs to understood in terms of spatial arrangements, but particularly in synagogues the exterior, or public, face is of less importance than the interior, sacred space.

No other book has ever shown so many views, exterior and interior, of so many synagogues.

These spaces, of course, really come alive when they are in use. Filled with people and the sounds of music and prayer, the architecture becomes fuller and richer. However, this is foremost a book about architecture, and we deliberately photographed these spaces without people in order to allow the greatest appreciation of the buildings themselves.

Carol Herselle Krinsky has written how synagogues "reveal especially clearly the connections between architecture and society."[2] The choices made in building synagogues can reveal much about the realities and the aspirations of Jewish communities at different times and in different places, and about different Jewish congregations coexisting at the same time and place. At no place and at no time is this truer than in twentieth-century America, which combines the fewest external restrictions on Jewish practice with the greatest demand.

Above: Chicago Loop Synagogue, Chicago, Illinois. The wall-size stained-glass window by Abraham Rattner.

# Chapter One

## House of Gathering

And let them make Me a sanctuary, that I may dwell among them. Exactly as I show you—the pattern of the Tabernacle and the pattern of all its furnishings—so you shall make it.

—Exodus 25:8–9

### The Nature of the Synagogue

For approximately a thousand years Judaism was a religion with a fixed center—Jerusalem—and a fixed architectural identity, the Temple. First built by King Solomon in the mid-tenth century B.C.E., the Temple was destroyed by the Babylonians in 586 B.C.E. and subsequently rebuilt. The new Temple was desecrated by Antiochus IV Epiphanes beginning in 169 B.C.E., which led to a Jewish revolt and the establishment of the Hasmonean dynasty—the event celebrated with the holiday of Hanukah. Finally, King Herod built a substantially new and expanded Temple complex on an enormous raised platform, beginning around 20 B.C.E.[1]

These structures, known collectively as the Second Temple, were destroyed by the Romans in 70 C.E. The date on which the Second Temple was destroyed was the same as that of the first, and ever since, the ninth day of Av has been a day of mourning and commemoration for Jews everywhere. There are no physical remains of any of the original Temples. Only the platform erected by Herod still stands, known to Jews as the Temple Mount and to Muslims as the Haram esh-Sharif (Noble Sanctuary). One portion of this platform—the Western, or Wailing, Wall—is especially venerated by Jews, who make pilgrimages to the site to pray. The wall has also become an architectural, as well as a religious icon, and its form is frequently referred to in contemporary synagogue design.

Since the destruction of the Second Temple, the synagogue has been the only truly Jewish contribution to world architecture. The synagogue, however, has been understood by most Jews over the centuries as a temporary replacement of the Temple. The Temple's "temporal architecture" has been translated to the synagogue, where prayer has replaced sacrifice.[2] But the synagogue has never been defined in architectural terms. A synagogue (from the Greek *synagein*, "to bring together") requires only an enclosed space to allow a congregation to assemble for worship and to hear the reading of the Torah (Five Books of Moses).[3]

The two most important elements of the interior of every synagogue are the *aron ha-kodesh* (Ark), which houses the Torah scrolls, and the *bimah*, or platform, from where the Torah is read aloud to the congregation. The prayer service creates a dynamic relationship between these elements. The synagogue must also include seating for the congregation and space for ceremonial processions, particularly when the Torah is taken from and returned to the Ark. Good sight lines and sufficient illumination, preferably by natural light, are desired. Seating can be arranged in many ways, though in Orthodox synagogues separate seating is required for women. This is often provided in a gallery, a solution used in 1675 in the Portuguese Synagogue in Amsterdam, which subsequently influenced the first American synagogues. Smaller spaces, however, can use any sort of barrier (*mehizah*) to divide women's and men's sections.[4]

The Jewish liturgy combines the regular and ordered reading and explanation of the Written Law, or Torah, to the community with prayers from the community to God. The Torah scroll, which contains the words

Opposite: Temple Beth Zion, Buffalo, New York. Stained-glass window by Ben Shahn, filling the wall behind the Ark and depicting Creation.

Above: Temple Brith Sholom, Cortland, New York. Views of Ark with curtain open and with curtain closed.

of God, is the holiest object in Jewish life. The Ark and *bimah*, because they are essential to the reading of the Torah and because they come in regular contact with the scroll, are the holiest parts of a synagogue.

Thus, the design of the Ark and *bimah* is given great attention by synagogue architects. The Ark is the central focus of the synagogue space. In the earliest synagogues, the Torah scrolls were kept in movable chests, which may have also served as readers' tables. These early Arks clearly related to the Holy Ark that was crafted by Bezalel and housed in the Tabernacle, erected under God's command in the wilderness of Sinai and described in the Book of Exodus (*Exodus* 32:1–5, 37:1–9). But soon it became accepted practice to place the Ark against the wall that faces Jerusalem. Though seating arrangements vary, worshippers almost always face the Ark (and hence Jerusalem) while praying.

By the late Roman and Byzantine periods (fifth through eighth centuries) apses and other architectural devices focused attention on the Ark. Numerous illustrations survive from the European Middle Ages showing the Ark as an ornate, freestanding cabinet. Building the Ark directly into the synagogue wall and elevating it a few steps above the main floor of the sanctuary became common by the sixteenth century.

The Ark is traditionally rectangular and made of wood, but it can be any size, shape, or material. In the twentieth century, artists and architects experimented with new materials, including glass and metal, and new shapes for the Ark. Some modern artists have created entirely original designs, but others have been inspired by the biblical description of Bezalel's Ark and other sources. The *bimah* can be a simple table, but it is usually more elaborate raised platform with a table, sometimes covered by a canopy of fabric, metal, or wood. The synagogue can contain other elements, too. These include decorative and symbolic lights, including an eternal light (*Ner tamid*) that stands before the Ark, and menorahs (seven-branched candelabra that recall the Menorah in the Jerusalem Temple).

Over time, a series of liturgical, architectural, and artistic solutions centered on the Ark and *bimah* have been adopted, creating arrangements that are immediately recognizable and quintessentially Jewish. Three basic spatial patterns dominate. In the Sephardic tradition, Ark and *bimah* are often placed at opposite ends of the room, and the congregation faces the axis between them. Congregants turn their heads from one to the other, as if the two furnishings were in dialogue. This is the form adopted by the earliest American congregations and still found at the established synagogues of congregations such as New York's Shearith Israel and Philadelphia's Mikveh Israel.

In traditional Ashkenazic (German and East European) synagogues the *bimah* is usually more centrally placed. The Torah reader—but not the rest of the congregation—maintains the dialogue with the Ark. In synagogues built on a centralized plan, such as the wooden synagogues in Poland, the centrally placed *bimah* creates a dynamic where the congregation encircles the reader. This tradition was preferred in the United States by most Eastern European immigrants in their first Orthodox congregations. The central *bimah* has remained essential in subsequent Orthodox synagogues, and has recently been revived in some Conservative synagogues, too, as in Congregation Agudath Achim in Austin, Texas.

Beginning in the nineteenth century, Reform Jews moved the *bimah* to the front of the Congregation immediately before the Ark, often creating a stagelike platform. The result is a more hierarchical arrangement that lends increased "decorum," which many nineteenth-century European and American Jews sought. In the twentieth century Conservative congregations also mostly moved the *bimah* up front. The inclusion or adaptation of this arrangement continues to challenge architects of American synagogues today.

### History of European Synagogues

The early rabbis who compiled the Talmud, the legal foundation of post-Temple Judaism, related the then new institution of the synagogue to the prophet Ezekiel's description of "lesser sanctuaries" that are temporary replacements for the Temple. In the post-Temple period, however, Jews have lavished attention on synagogues when opportunity allowed. The size and architecture of many synagogues are intended to suggest permanence, even though the facts of Jewish history have instead made most synagogues temporary. Centuries of oppression in Europe and prosperity in the United States have both led to the abandonment and destruction of thousands of synagogues.[5]

Synagogues did not replace the Jewish Temple—the locus of Jewish worship in antiquity. The functions of the Temple and the synagogue are fundamentally different—ritual sacrifice for the former, prayer for the latter. Thus, the architecture of the synagogue also differs from the Temple. In the nineteenth century, many Reform Jews in Europe and the United States rejected Jewish yearning for a return to Israel in the time of the Messiah, and chose to identify more fully with their Diaspora homelands. Consequently, they began to call their modern synagogues "temples"—though imitation of the ancient Jerusalem cult was not intended, these synagogues were often big, prominent, and lavishly decorated.

There have developed over a long period of time, however, certain parallels between Temple and synagogue, many of which are encoded into the liturgy. Prayer services at synagogue correlate to the times of offering at the Temple, and the separation of men and women in Orthodox synagogues derives from Temple regulations. Other relations are symbolic: physical reminders of the standing Temple, such as the incorporation of two columns or turrets, which may represent the brazen columns from Solomon's Temple described in the book of Kings and named, for still unknown reasons, Jakhin and Boaz; the covering of the Ark with a curtain recalls the veil of the Holy of Holies. There are sometimes reminders of the Temple's destruction, such as part of a wall left unplastered when synagogues are built. Associations exist, too, between the synagogue's Ark (*aron ha-kodesh*) and the Ark of the Covenant (*aron ha-birit*), which Solomon placed in the Holy of Holies in the Temple. Though the two Arks (the Hebrew word means "chest") have very different functions—one is where God resided, and the other is where the Torah, or Word of God, is housed—they are linked in most Jews' minds. Some architects and artists, such as Philip Trammel Shutze at Atlanta's Temple, have emphasized this connection.

Early on in the history of the Diaspora, the multipurpose synagogue became the center of Jewish life and community identity. Since antiquity synagogues have been frequently used for community assemblies and legal proceedings, and as religious study houses. Synagogues were, until recently, the focus of most Jewish artistic endeavors because broader cultural and artistic expression was forbidden or at least discouraged by the laws of the cultural majority as well as by Jewish law and tradition.

In Europe, community synagogues did not stand in isolation. They were often surrounded by a host of communal buildings including a rabbi's house, a communal office, a social hall, school, and *mikveh* (ritual bath). In modern times a Jewish community may also operate a hospital, a nursing home, and other social welfare facilities. These are not, however, distinctly Jewish in character, although they sometimes contain a small synagogue for use by residents or patients. In the United States, Jews are free to choose their religious institutions, to congregate as they please, and there are no official Jewish communities requiring registration and taxation. Synagogues are founded by like-minded congregants who define their own religious identity. Thus, most American synagogues prior to 1900 consisted of only a building for prayer. The Jewish community used other facilities to meet their various needs.

Increasingly, congregations have added non-worship facilities such as schools, libraries, offices, kitchens, social halls, gymnasiums, and so on, to their synagogues to attract and serve their members. The result is the "synagogue center," which takes on the multifunctional role of the ancient synagogue.[6] The need for the synagogue center increased as the cohesion of Jewish neighborhoods declined.

Throughout the world, until the nineteenth century, by choice or circumstance, Jewish structures only occasionally rivaled Christian or civic architecture in size or decoration. There was no state or royal sponsorship and no extensive land holdings to finance construction. Laws promulgated by Christian and Muslim rulers limited the size and appearance of synagogues. Nonetheless, given the opportunity to build, Jews often did so. In the American colonies Jewish communities were able to afford attractive buildings, but the small size of early congregations made large buildings unnecessary, and sensitivity to their own history and to the cultural mores of the surrounding society compelled congregations to avoid ostentatious displays.

Not all synagogues, however, are architecturally distinctive. Many Jewish congregations, especially when new and poor, have merely adapted existing spaces with few changes. Most American Jewish congregations began in rented rooms above a store, in a private house, or in an unused Protestant church, and this process continues today.

### Interior Plans

Interior plans for synagogues take many forms. The basilica plan—with a wide central aisle often terminating in a projecting apse and narrower side aisles—has been popular. It is inherited from Roman architecture and is also used for Christian churches. Multi-aisle synagogues were common in antiquity and in medieval Spain. The basilica's side aisles could be curtained off for women, but its decidedly longitudinal and hierarchical form was not well suited for traditional Jewish worship.

The hall plan, which is simply an open, usually rectangular room with no columnar obstructions, is often preferred, especially for smaller congregations. Hall plans are usually of modest dimensions because of the structural limitations of roof spans. Private synagogues, often attached to or within a patron's house, took this form. The interior spaces of hall-plan synagogues are often exceptionally tall, with space to insert galleries for women along two or three sides of the room. Upper galleries maximized the seating capacity and created a theatrical atmosphere, which has often been heightened by the application of rich decoration throughout, as in Italian synagogues from the sixteenth century and later. The verticality of hall-plan interiors is often wholly unexpected from the outside.

In medieval Germany and Central Europe a double-nave consisting of a vaulted space divided into two equal aisles by a central row of columns or piers, was frequently adopted. This had the symbolic advantage of being quite distinct from a medieval church, but it was inadequate because the columns obstructed sight lines to the Ark, which was on the same axis. To minimize this problem the entrances were placed at oblique angles to the Ark, and benches were set around the periphery of the space to allow broad sight lines. The worshipers faced the central *bimah* more than the Ark.

The use of lighter wood construction and of improved masonry vaulting after the sixteenth century allowed the development of broader, loftier interiors. In Poland a new vaulted hall type created some of the most magnificent synagogue interiors ever built. The central plan, wide-open space, and high ceiling also encouraged the development of increasingly ornate *bimahs*, which often copied in smaller form the plan of the synagogue. The Polish wooden synagogues, all destroyed during World War II, were the highest expression of this type of design.

In the nineteenth century, Reform congregations developed a new form of interior articulation that closely followed traditional church architecture. This arrangement has come to dominate American synagogue design. Reformers adopted more "propriety" in the worship service, with less spontaneous prayer, and more united responses. Synagogues were arranged more for performers (clergy) and audience (congregation) than for prayer leaders and participants. Some older synagogues also had this arrangement, but on a smaller scale. The *bimah* was moved from the center of the space to immediately in front of or to the side of the Ark. A single set of steps now led to the enlarged platform, and all ritual and reading was centralized on this single space. Pulpits were also added, since preaching and sermons by rabbis, often in the vernacular language or in German, became an important part of the public service. Galleries continued in use in this type of building, sometimes rising in two levels. In Europe separate seating for men and women was maintained in many Reform synagogues, and mixed seating was only gradually adopted.[7]

In much of Central and Eastern Europe, separate space for female congregants had usually been in annexes, connected to the main space of these hall-plan synagogues with small windows. Galleries in the sanctuaries began to be designed around 1600. By the eighteenth century, in buildings such as the Touro Synagogue in Newport, Rhode Island, upper-level galleries for women wrapped around three sides of the space. This arrangement, always popular in urban areas because it allowed maximum seating in a limited area, was until recently particularly popular in synagogues in the United States.

Adequate seating for women in the American synagogue has not been a high concern for architects, since the majority of synagogues they designed in the twentieth century were for Reform or Conservative congregations, which allow mixed seating. Most Orthodox synagogues of the nineteenth century, such as Shearith Israel in New York, had galleries. The growth of congregations, the increased demand for seating space, and the often restricted space available for building new urban synagogues, had combined to keep galleries essential for most Orthodox and Reform congregations, despite their shortcomings. In 1909, however, William Tachau designed a new synagogue for the venerated

Congregation Mikveh Israel in Philadelphia, which as an Orthodox Sephardic synagogue maintained the separation of the sexes. Describing his design, Tachau wrote:

> Here it was decided that it was too much of a physical hardship for the women to climb to a high gallery, so the old idea of stationing the women's section near the ground level was revived. It is arranged on either side of the building, and can easily be reached be a few steps leading from the common vestibule, which lies in front of the hall of worship.[8]

This innovation was used much later in the design of the Orthodox Sons of Israel in Lakewood, New Jersey.

### Synagogue Decoration

Synagogues have always been decorated. We know from archaeological excavations that even the ancient synagogues had elaborate floor mosaics, and at least some had wall paintings. Some of these decorations were geometric and filled with inscriptions. Others included symbolic and decorative devices common in ancient art that derived directly from pagan religious sources. In the wall paintings at Dura-Europas (third century) and the floor mosaics at Beth Alpha (sixth century), artists depicted human figures as part of narrative action. Most of these decorations were unknown until the twentieth century but their rediscovery greatly influenced the design and decoration of modern synagogues.

Medieval *responsa* (the written opinions of rabbis in response to thorny questions of Jewish law and practice) discuss the type of decoration allowed in synagogues. Surviving fragments and pre–World War II photographs demonstrate how lavish and how fanciful such decoration could be.

Synagogues have long contained richly decorated textiles and elaborately carved and painted arks and *bimahs*. Stained glass was used in congregations that agreed to its appropriateness. In Muslim countries brightly colored tiles and ornate stuccowork decorate synagogues while following the proscriptions against representation art in Islam. In all cases, Hebrew calligraphy, used for dedicatory inscriptions, inspirational biblical passages, or the transcription of whole prayers, also served as decoration. This tradition has been continued in modern American synagogues. One of the most exceptional examples of calligraphic art was created by Sigmund Wolpert at Sons of Israel in Lakewood, New Jersey. Inscriptions also play important instructional and aesthetic roles at Norman Jaffe's Jewish Center of the Hamptons in East Hampton, New York, and at Alexander Gorlin's North Shore Hebrew Academy Synagogue in King's Point, New York.

The Second Commandment has often been cited as a prohibition against art in Judaism, including synagogue decoration, based on an extremely narrow interpretation of the passage in Deuteronomy 5:8–9, that reads, "You shall not make for yourself a graven image or any likeness. . . . You shall not bow down to them or serve them." [9] Too often the commandment has been understood as a restriction of art, rather than a prohibition of idolatry.[10] Evidence from other scriptural passages, especially the descriptions of the building of the Tabernacle, and later of the Temple in Jerusalem show that artistic expression was an accepted part of the Jewish religious experience. Exodus 15:2, "This is my God and I will glorify Him," has generated the concept of "Beauty in Holiness," which encourages the elaboration of places and objects that facilitate worship of God and the teaching of God's laws. The physical evidence of past synagogues and Jewish ritual objects supports this view.

Modern rabbis, especially Reform rabbis, have championed art in the synagogue, including figural art of an explicit nature not known since the frescoes were painted at the synagogue of Dura-Europas. Rabbi Edgar Magnin of the Wilshire Boulevard Temple in Los Angeles enthusiastically supported the painted frieze in that synagogue that narrates Jewish history. Rabbi Philip Bernstein of B'rith Kodesh in Rochester defended the bronze Ark in that synagogue that represents in expressive, but clearly figural, form, scriptural accounts of patriarchs' and prophets' encounters with God. Modern artists who have created work for synagogues, such as Abraham Rattner, Ibram Lassow, and Louise Nevelson, often use less explicit, abstract forms to tell the story of creation or to represent various attributes of God or Jewish virtues.

Opposite: Temple B'rith Kodesh, Rochester, New York. Sanctuary from the rear.

# Chapter Two

## Jews in America: Older Traditions in a New Homeland

Happy are those who dwell in your house; they for ever praise You.

—Psalms 84:5

Jews left Europe for new homes in three main waves. In the sixteenth and seventeenth centuries, Spanish (Sephardic) Jews and their descendants settled in many New World and Asian ports along the developing trade routes. In some places, usually under Dutch or English rule, they flourished. A small but prosperous Sephardic Jewish population in the U.S. participated in the War of Independence. These Jews founded synagogues in five cities—Philadelphia; New York; Newport, Rhode Island; Charleston, South Carolina; and Savannah, Georgia—before 1800.

In the mid-nineteenth century, thousands of Central European Jews were part of the mass emigration to the United States caused by political unrest and economic instability in Europe. Despite improvements for many European Jews after the Napoleonic era, Jews from Germany, France (Alsace), Bohemia, and elsewhere sought a better life in the United States. Many of these immigrants became commercial pioneers, starting as peddlers, and eventually settled in hundreds of towns throughout the American South and West. They played a pivotal role in the expansion of the American frontier and the cohesion of the new nation. Many eventually abandoned Judaism, but others formed small communities, built synagogues, and continued traditions. Substantial communities of "German" Jews were established in many cities, including some with earlier Sephardic congregations. In Charleston, Philadelphia, and New York new congregations were founded—differentiating American Jews for the first time as Sephardic and Ashkenazic.[1] New Jewish centers, such as Cincinnati (the country's biggest city after New York), were important in developing American Judaism in this period.

As early as 1824 in Charleston, however, some American Jews began to transform the centuries-old ritual and worship practices of the Old World. Many of these changes were practical, given the paucity of trained rabbis and religious teachers in the new republic. Gradually, however, such practical changes, which included the more frequent use of vernacular languages in the service (first German, then English), shortening the service by eliminating some prayer repetitions, the introduction of music, especially organ music, and eventually mixed seating for men and women, coalesced into what is now known as Reform Judaism. American Reform developed naturally in an environment of newfound freedoms, where Jews were a small, relatively isolated minority. In Europe, on the other hand, the Reform movement was largely the result of a real need to conform to Christian standards to win social and political acceptance. Thus, the changes championed by European reformers tended to be more integrated and ideological than in the U.S., but the European rationale for Reform was eventually grafted on to American practice, leading to a fairly unified American Reform movement with its own rabbinic seminary, Hebrew Union College, established in Cincinnati in 1875.

The third wave of immigration from Europe—by far the biggest—occurred in the late nineteenth century. Millions of Jews—approximately a third of the Jewish population—fled Eastern Europe, particularly those territories controlled by Russia and repressed under tsarist rule. From the 1880s to the 1920s more than a million Jews from Poland and Russia settled in North America. The Jewish population in the United States increased from 250,000 in 1880 to over four million in 1920.

Before 1880 and the beginning of mass Jewish immigration from Eastern Europe, Reform Judaism was widespread and growing in America, with special strength in the South and West. New Orthodox immigrants,

Opposite: Congregation Emanu-El of the City of New York, New York. The rear of the Romanesque-style Beth El Chapel, dedicated in 1931.

however, confronted the Reform establishment and within a generation created a countermovement: Conservative Judaism. Conservative Judaism remained traditional, but accepted many realities of modern life and incorporated them into its religious and communal practice. Increased use of English in the service, mixed seating, relaxation of Sabbath restrictions on driving to synagogue, and the use of electricity and other conveniences were some of the many changes. The Conservative movement competed effectively with Reform Judaism, especially among newer immigrant families. In the first half of the twentieth century, Conservative Judaism grew quickly as it became the main route for the Americanization of second-generation Eastern European Jews. The Jewish Theological Seminary, established in New York in 1887 and reorganized in 1902, trained rabbis for Conservative congregations, and gradually increased uniformity throughout the movement. By mid-century Reform and Conservative congregations dominated the face of American Judaism.

Since the 1950s still more Jewish immigrants have come to the United States, particularly from North Africa, Syria, and Iran. These groups have formed coherent communities with new synagogue congregations, mostly in New York and Los Angeles.

### The First American Synagogues

The earliest reference to a synagogue in North America is the indication on a map of New York drawn in 1695 by John Miller.[2] On September 8, 1729, four cornerstones were laid according to the tradition of the Great Synagogue of the Portuguese Jews in Amsterdam, and New York's Mill Street Synagogue (the complex also included a schoolhouse, a ritual bath, a well, and a pump) was dedicated the following April.[3]

At Mill Street, women occupied a gallery with, as one contemporary observer noted, "a breastwork as high as their chins."[4] Galleries were standard in American churches, but the separation of men and women was not—though it was traditional in synagogues. In the women's gallery at Mill Street a *banco* (bench) was reserved in the northwest corner of the main floor for the ladies of the Gomez family, prominent members of the congregation. When this privileged pew was removed after the Revolution, in 1786, the front bench was extended for all married women and others who represented families. Thus began, at a very early date, the gradual process of democratization and integration of the sexes in the seating of American synagogues. Seating arrangements have changed considerably throughout the past two centuries, and adjustments continue to be made within the norms established by all branches of Judaism.

American synagogue architecture until World War II mostly followed American Christian architecture, but specific influences from European synagogues have also been felt. New printing technologies introduced in the mid-nineteenth century—when European congregations were erecting architecturally ambitious synagogues—allowed magazines to print color images. Jewish congregations in the U.S. often hired leading architects to adapt the European designs they saw in magazines, or to devise their own new buildings to rival the achievements of the Old Country.[5]

Nineteenth-century European Jews often rejected the established Christian architectural styles, particularly the Gothic. Christian authorities, while supporting the erection of large synagogues, often insisted that they differ architecturally from churches. Thus, architecture became an important element in the debate over Jewish assimilation. Both Greek and Roman temple styles became acceptable alternatives for synagogues during this period, serving as an intermediary style. Many non-Jewish architects and public authorities wanted a distinct Jewish architectural style or form to clearly distinguish Jewish buildings from Christian. The Moorish style, which combined Byzantine, Arab, and Oriental motifs, first appeared in a synagogue at Dresden (1838–40), built by Gottfried Semper, and soon swept the major cities of Central Europe with massive examples in Vienna (1853–58), Budapest (1854–59), Berlin (1859–66), and elsewhere. The style was never employed for churches in Europe, and only seldom in the United States. Contrary to popular notions, Sephardic congregations, with origins in Spain, never used this style.

American Jews inherited this mixed legacy. Sephardic Jews, who emigrated via Holland, were already accustomed to classicism—as demonstrated in a series of synagogues built from the sixteenth through the eighteenth centuries in Venice, Amsterdam, London, Surinam, Curaçao, and St. Thomas. None of these buildings emulated pagan temples but they did use classically inspired elements, such as columns, which were especially popular during Renaissance-Baroque architectural revivals.

In the United States, Jewish communities employed classical traditions in the first Sephardic synagogues. Examples include the subdued Georgian classicism of Peter Harrison's Touro Synagogue in Newport, Rhode Island (1753); the mix of Classicism and Egyptian Revival at Mikveh Israel Synagogue of Philadelphia (1824–25), designed by William Strickland; and the Greek Revival synagogues erected by Shearith Israel in New York (1834); Beth Elohim in Charleston (second building, 1841); and the Baltimore Hebrew Congregation in Baltimore (1845, known as the Lloyd Street Synagogue).[6] The Greek Revival synagogues were based on the popular Greek temple form, with exterior colonnades, an emphasis on the exterior of the building infrequently employed by Jews since antiquity.

The Touro Synagogue, designed by Peter Harrison, in Newport still stands and remains in use. Though of modest size, the elegant building is equal in quality to the finest contemporary civic structures in the colonies. Though it is often compared to the Portuguese Synagogue in Amsterdam, there is little similarity between the two. Harrison's more important source was English contemporary design, which he would have known from architectural handbooks.[7] Synagogue architects of the time employed contemporary architectural vocabulary as a reflection of the cultural taste of their Jewish patrons, who thoroughly embraced the standards of the day. (Jews were relatively few in number and many doors remained closed to them, but they were well represented in the economic and cultural elite.) The use of contemporary style sometimes reduced a synagogue's distinctiveness, as in the first building of Charleston's Beth Elohim, built in 1794 with a prominent steeple that made it look like a church.

Jews even experimented with the Egyptian Revival, another style popular in the nineteenth century. Mikveh Israel Synagogue of Philadelphia, designed by William Strickland, and the Crown Street synagogue (1849, now demolished), also in Philadelphia and designed by Thomas U. Walter, were both in this style. It is curious, but not surprising given regular communication in the Jewish (and English-speaking) world, that communities as distant as the United States, Australia, and Scandinavia chose similar Egyptian Revival designs.[8]

There are notable exceptions to general trends. Although the traditional Gothic style, so popular in church architecture, was not frequently used for urban synagogues, a vernacular Gothic, practiced by local carpenters and masons, was common for small-town congregations, especially in the West from the 1840s to the 1880s. An example of this was the first new building erected for Los Angeles's Congregation B'nai Brith, built in 1873.[9] The congregation moved twice thereafter and was later housed in the Wilshire Boulevard Temple (chapter 4).

The Moorish style was embraced by first-generation German Jews who arrived in the United States in the 1840s but became prosperous enough to build large synagogues only from about 1860. Examples such as the Plum Street Synagogue in Cincinnati (1866); Central Synagogue, New York (1872); Oheb Shalom, Newark, New Jersey (1884); Eldridge St. Synagogue, New York (1886); or the tiny Gemilleth Chassid in Port Gibson, Mississippi (1891) can be still seen. Most of the opulent synagogues built in this style, however, have been demolished, replaced by more subdued, often classical, structures.

By the late nineteenth century increasingly assimilated Jews found the Moorish style too exotic, un-American, and old-fashioned. Only a few Moorish-style synagogues, such as the Orthodox B'nai Abraham (1910) at Sixth and Lombard Streets in Philadelphia, were built after this time. After 1900 classicism and its variants were the styles of the day.

MY·HOUSE·SHALL·BE·CALLED·A·HOUSE·OF·PRAYER·FOR·ALL·PEOPLE·

# Chapter Three

## A Jewish-American Renaissance: High Style Architecture (1900–1914)

My house shall be called a house of prayer for all people.

—Isaiah 56:7

In the late nineteenth century, American Judaism, especially the Reform Movement, underwent a crisis. Americanization of Jews had been so thorough that attendance at synagogues, including many that had been lavishly and expensively erected in the previous generation, had fallen precipitously. Rabbis castigated their congregations from their pulpits with little or no effect.

In 1885 Rabbi Emil Hirsch called leading Reform rabbis—many of whom were among the first graduates in 1883 from the Hebrew Union College—to Pittsburgh. This historic conference adopted what came to be known as the Pittsburgh Platform, which set a new agenda for Reform Judaism in the United States It expanded synagogue activity beyond religious services so that congregations would be more fully and regularly engaged in activities—religious, educational, social, and political—that emphasized Jewish life. At the same time, the platform reiterated the openness of Reform Judaism and its fundamentally American nature.

Over the next two decades as these plans took effect across the country, new directions were introduced into synagogue buildings. Thus, in addition to stylistic change that was the result of both social and aesthetic forces, certain functional changes also began to dominate synagogue design.

### Jewish Classicism

During the same period, American architectural and artistic taste underwent a dramatic course adjustment due to the popularity of the Chicago Columbian Exposition of 1893. The Exposition, which was dubbed the "White City" because of its Neoclassical architecture, inspired a period known for its enthusiasm for Classical and Renaissance artistic models, the often lavish patronage of artists and architects, and extensive building programs, especially of public structures such as town halls, courthouses, and religious buildings. Until the First World War thousands of white (and gray) buildings with columns and domes were erected across America. Greek Classicism had helped define the values of the early republic. Now, during the "American Renaissance," a full-bodied Roman Classicism reflected the values of the new American empire. Synagogues that superficially resembled Roman temples began to be erected across the country.

Although we now know through archaeological excavation about hundreds of synagogues scattered throughout the ancient world, little of this information was available when the early classical-style synagogues were built. It was less the Jewish past than the American present that informed and influenced synagogue patrons or architects. Though they used classical elements such as columns and pediments, ancient synagogues had not been built in the form of Greek or Roman temples. Early Jewish (and Christian) religious buildings were closer in form to Roman secular architecture. They emphasized interior space rather than exterior articulation. Jews abhorred paganism and rejected its architecture—this is what the holiday of Hanukkah is all about.

At least one prominent and prolific American synagogue architect, however, was aware of the new discoveries. Arnold W. Brunner (1857–1925) wrote about these finds and justified his own use of classical forms for synagogue design by citing the archaeological record. Brunner, who before 1893 had designed several New York synagogues in a mix of Romanesque and Moorish styles, erected his first classical syna-

Opposite: Congregation Rodef Shalom, Pittsburgh, Pennsylvania.

Below: Temple Society of Concord, Syracuse, New York. The 1910 classical façade from the northwest. With this building, designed by leading classical architect Arnold Brunner, the congregation (the ninth oldest in the U.S.) indicated full acceptance of the City Beautiful ideals of the time.

gogue shortly after the Chicago "White City" closed. Brunner's Shearith Israel in New York was dedicated in 1897, and immediately set a high standard for classical synagogue design.

Brunner was born in New York City to a German-Jewish family, and graduated from the Massachusetts Institute of Technology. In addition to Shearith Israel, he also designed New York's Beth El synagogue and later major buildings at Columbia University as well as government buildings in Harrisburg, Pennsylvania; Cleveland; Ohio, and elsewhere.

Archaeological finds and the popularity of classicism certainly inspired Brunner's work at Shearith Israel, but there was also a specific historic precedent for his design. Shearith Israel, the nation's oldest Jewish congregation, had for 150 years favored classical designs.[1] Its second synagogue at Crosby Street (1834) resembled a small Greek Temple, and its third building on West 19th Street (1860) reflected Roman Baroque designs of the early seventeenth century.[2] In a sense, Brunner's design for the new building on Central Park West at 70th Street was a compromise between these two earlier buildings. His monumental facade recalled 19th Street, but the more restrained classicism he used inside echoed the Crosby Street building. The new building thus captures the congregation's passion for preserving its own history. It even includes a small chapel that re-creates in part the two earlier Sheareth Israel synagogues. Built to the same dimensions as the earlier buildings, it uses many features and furnishings that had been saved by the congregation from its earliest homes.

The facade is a Roman temple front with two levels of arched openings. Above this is a heavy cornice topped by a pediment. All the arched bays are framed by tall Corinthian columns, the first use of this motif in an American synagogue. The building sits on a corner site so the adjacent facade is also articulated with care—three extremely tall arched windows are framed with Corinthian pilasters. The corners of the building appear more solid, as massive piers buttressing the open arched walls.

The interior of the synagogue is virtually square, 69 by 70 feet, but it appears rectangular because of the galley seating arrangement. Two banks of seats along the "long" walls face an open space or well in the center of the building. The Ark and *bimah* are at opposite ends of the interior. Keeping with Jewish tradition, Brunner placed the Ark against the east wall, but since this is also the main facade wall, he ingeniously rotated the interior design from what one might expect in a classical building. That is, the focal point of interior attention is the entrance wall.

Soon after, Brunner designed a second classically inspired synagogue that was more specifically dependent on ancient synagogue sources: the Frank Memorial Synagogue for the Jewish Hospital of Philadelphia, completed in 1901. Brunner drew explicitly on an ancient Jewish model, the large fourth-century C.E. synagogue of Kefar Baram ("Kfir Birim" in Arabic) in what is now northern Israel—a building that had been made known by the Palestine Exploration Fund.[3]

In a 1907 article Brunner explained his preference for the classical style:

> Some years ago, when what was known as the "Richardson Romanesque" was apparently becoming the expression of American ecclesiastical architecture, it seemed that in a slightly modified form it would be appropriate for the synagogue. When I built the Temple Beth El in New York I so believed. After Richardson's death, when his methods were not successfully continued by his followers and imitators, the Romanesque practically disappeared and the choice for architects by now, broadly speaking, lies between the two great styles, Gothic and classic. I am unhesitatingly of the opinion that the latter is the one that is fit and proper for the synagogue in America. With the sanction of antiquity it perpetuates the best traditions of Jewish art and takes up a thread, which was broken by circumstances, of a vigorous and once healthy style.[4]

Brunner's precepts can also be observed in the former Temple Israel in Harlem (now Mount Olivet Baptist Church) and Temple Society of Concord in Syracuse, New York, where he was the consulting architect.

## Temple Society of Concord
## Syracuse, New York
Arnold Brunner
1910



Temple Society of Concord contains most of the signature elements of Brunner's style. The building is overtly classical, from its hilltop setting to its solemn Doric columns, which convey a massive majesty beyond the building's size. Both exterior and interior are devoid of architectural and decorative clutter so that important details, such as the Greek key design in the triumphal arch above the Ark and *bimah,* stand out. The proportions and acoustics of the sanctuary are good, and the full windows on either side flood the space with daylight, welcoming both group prayer and quiet contemplation.[5]

The Syracuse Reform congregation is one of the oldest in the United States, and its history is fairly typical of many American congregations. Founded in 1839 by German-speaking immigrants drawn to upstate New York by the new Erie Canal, the small group first met in the back room of a local store. Like so many other American congregations, they soon moved to better quarters, first to the second floor of a member's home on Mulberry Street, where by 1841 they hired their first rabbi (although he was not formally trained or ordained). The minyan incorporated and took the name Keneseth Shalome, which was later changed to the Temple Society of Concord. In 1851 the congregation built its own building at Harrison and Mulberry Streets for the substantial sum of $10,000.

The new building exacerbated conflict over identity and religious practice within the congregation, and led members in 1861 to adopt Reform Judaism, the growing movement led by Rabbi Isaac Wise of Cincinnati. Thus, in addition to certain formal changes in the synagogue layout, the congregation allowed the inclusion of an organ, choir singing, family pews, and English translations of prayers. When the synagogue president required that men remove their hats in the synagogue—in direct opposition of traditional Jewish practice, a large faction split from Temple Concord and founded its own synagogue. Despite the split, Temple Concord continued to grow, expanding its activities especially in the area of religious and Hebrew education, as urged by the Pittsburgh Convention of 1885. True to the pro-assimilation teachings of Reform Judaism, this was done within a distinctly American context. As Rabbi Adolph Guttman, who led the congregation for thirty-six years, stated,

Right: The ample sanctuary is well-lit, comfortable, and dignified without ostentation—all hallmarks of Brunner's late style.

"In our religion we are Jews, but in every other respect we are part and parcel of this great country, which we love with heart and mind. Its flag is our flag, it victories our victories, its defeats our defeats."[6]

By 1910 the congregation was ready to move into its new classical building, completed in the best American manner for $100,000 as a "temple on the hill." The facade, reached by a long flight of steps, consists of a portico of four columns screening three sets of double doors. Above the central entryway is the English inscription, "Mine house shall be called an [*sic*] house of prayer for all peoples." (Isaiah 56:7) Set above each of the other doors is the Star of David—the only external ornament that indicates the building's Jewish identity.

A tiny vestibule inside the main doors opens onto a long, wide, open hall filled with natural light by rows of tall windows along each side. A flat, coffered ceiling with minimal decoration surmounts the space. The acoustics allow a good voice or choir to easily project through the entire sanctuary. From the original entrance, the eye is drawn immediately to the far end where a simple, slightly flattened, triumphal arch surmounts the raised *bimah* and Ark. The Ark itself is classically severe, but small enough not to be imposing. Like the details at the Frank synagogue in Philadelphia, this Ark recalls ancient synagogues. In fact, Brunner would be vindicated as the decades passed and more archaeological remains came to light. For example, the Ark at the third-century C.E. synagogue in Sardis, Turkey, bears a striking resemblance to that at Temple Society of Concord.

Following Brunner's lead, the strong trend toward classicism and structural and decorative integration led to the notable Beth Ahabah, in Richmond, Virginia, built by Noland & Baskerville (1904); Mikveh Israel in Philadelphia designed by William Tachau and Lewis Pilcher (1909); Temple Emanuel in Birmingham, Alabama (1914); and scores of similar buildings erected across the country. Anshe Sholom (Alexander Levy, 1910) and Sinai Temple (Alfred S. Alschuler, 1909–12, now demolished) exemplified the style in Chicago.

Among the finest classical synagogues is Detroit's Beth El Congregation, designed by Albert Kahn (1869–1942), a member of the congregation. Beth El, built in 1903 at Woodward Avenue between Erskine and Eliot Streets, is now a theater. It was designed with a columnar portico and pediment entrance leading to an octagonal interior surmounted by a saucer dome clearly influenced by the Pantheon, a building Kahn admired. (A large photo of the Roman temple hung over Kahn's office desk.)[7] Inside Beth El, however, the style is less restrained, with plentiful plaster cartouches and other embellishments. The Ark was set into the center of a huge wooden wall, built in two levels. The top level contained the pipes of the mighty organ. This Ark wall was classically articulated with columns and architraves. Seating ranged outward from the raised *bimah* in semicircular rows of benches. Thus, sight lines to the Ark and *bimah* were fairly good from every seat.

A large assembly room was located on the same floor as the sanctuary. The two spaces were separated by a lobby. The assembly room, in turn, was connected to classrooms, a library, and a corridor leading to men's and women's parlors. This arrangement—sanctuary and assembly room /social hall opposed across a lobby space—became the norm in synagogue architecture after World War II. The use of folding doors to connect spaces was known earlier (in the lower level of the 1876 Adas Israel in Washington, D.C., for example, and in the small Temple Beth El in Tyler, Texas, built in the 1930s by Howard R. Meyer and Charles J. Pete, where folding doors separate the sanctuary from the social hall.) Kahn's Beth El design takes the idea further, without, however, including folding doors to connect the sanctuary with the assembly hall. This arrangement would be further developed by Percival Goodman in the 1940s and 1950s.[8]

Balconies flanked the sanctuary to accommodate overflow crowds. Because this was a Reform synagogue, women sat with men in the main hall. The functionality of the interior layout indicates that Kahn applied to the synagogue the same rational principles he used in his successful factory designs. Indeed, in the same year that Beth El was constructed, Kahn designed his Packard Motor Company Factory and thus launched his career as the foremost designer of industrial spaces in the world. Here, however, because of the nature of the commission, the vocabulary of the building is a dignified classicism.

In addition to synagogues, numerous public buildings of the time featured a central dome. For synagogues and churches, domes could be interpreted as the vault of heaven. One of the reasons impressive domes became so popular was a new and relatively inexpensive building technology—Guastovino vaulting. This adaptation of a traditional Catalan masonry technique was introduced into the United States and patented

Above: Brunner, like many architects of the time, employed an ancient Greco-Roman temple form to house a modern Jewish Temple. The well-proportioned façade looks west toward downtown Syracuse.

by Rafael Guastavino. His company went on to vault more than a thousand notable structures across the country, including Low Memorial Library at Columbia University (which inspired many synagogues), Grand Central Terminal, Carnegie Hall, Ellis Island, the U.S. Supreme Court building, and the Boston Public Library. Guastavino's domes of beautiful, laminated tiles helped revolutionize architecture in the United States and were an important factor in the popularity and affordability of the classical style of the American Renaissance.[9] A Guastavino dome can be seen at Pittsburgh's Rodef Shalom. The interior walls of New York's Temple Emanu-El (chapter 4) are clad in Guastavino acoustic tile.

It is possible that congregations associated their columnar facades with the Temple in Jerusalem, described in the Bible as having two columns, called Jachin and Boaz, flanking the main portal (I Kings 7:21). This connection, however, was never overt.[10] Until the advent of the Reform movement in the early nineteenth century, Jews were averse to comparing synagogues (which were viewed as temporary sanctuaries) with the Temple. And because a large number of contemporary structures, including churches and custom houses, also utilized the Greek temple form, it could be that Jews were being fashionable, not symbolic, in their choice of style. Jewish communities felt secure and accepted. The architectural designs, often commissioned from the leading architects of the day, reflected this Jewish integration into the affairs of the new nation.

Left: The classically designed Ark is bedecked with Jewish symbols. An eternal light hangs from a Star of David in the pediment; the words "Holy to the Lord" are inscribed in Hebrew on the frieze; and large menorahs stand at either side.

### The Classical Style in the Midwest

Soon after the Columbian Exposition of 1893, Chicago began to see synagogues incorporate classical elements and eventually fully classical designs. The latter included Temple Israel (St. Lawrence and 44th Street, 1898), Southside Hebrew Congregation (35th St. and Indiana Ave., 1901), and Temple Emanuel (Buckingham Place between Halsted St. and Broadway, 1908).[11] It was Alexander Levy's Anshe Sholom, however, built at Ashland Avenue and Polk Street and dedicated in 1910, that fully articulated the classical taste of the time.

The large synagogue was fronted with a tall portico of four Corinthian columns, surmounted by a pediment, capped with a Star of David. The synagogue occupies a corner, and the south wall consists of wide, tall arched windows set above a high half-basement. These prominent elements are articulated as a podium on which the "temple" synagogue sits. The roof, surrounded by a parapet wall, is surmounted by an octagonal drum topped with a domed cupola. A Serliana motif of small columns supporting arches adorns the cupola.[12]

Other than Brunner and Kahn, two of the most effective practitioners of the classical style in synagogue architecture, and among the most prolific, were William Tachau (1875–1969), originally of St. Louis, and Alfred S. Alschuler (1876–1940). Alschuler, a Chicagoan, designed Sinai Temple in Chicago in 1909 (completed 1912) in what he termed, "free Renaissance chiefly of the Italian School, adapted to our purposes."[13] The building's fine proportions, detailing, and use of Bedford limestone facing give it an important, official appearance resembling a library or museum. The orientation of the building, which places the long side of the synagogue's rectangular plan along the street, is unusual. Alschuler claimed this solution was dictated by the narrowness of the lot, but it also well served the interior, whose amphitheater arrangement brings every seat much closer to the *bimah* and Ark than in a traditional longitudinal basilica plan.

According to Alschuler, "The interior decorations [were] kept in a simple neutral tone in order to bring out the detail and lines of the building and to produce the most restful and at the same time spiritual effects."[14] At the top of a flight of wide exterior stairs a recessed entryway behind a screen of columns heightens the sense of pomp. Inside, the space is one huge hall, unbroken by any dividers or supports. The broad vault with three rectangular skylights spans an area of open theater seating. A balcony rings threes sides of the space.

Alschuler created several less ambitious synagogues in the Chicago area that derive from the Sinai design, notably the Georgian style Temple Sholom and B'nai Sholom Temple Israel.[15] In these, however, he shifted the orientation so that one enters from the short side, as is more common. Both buildings were faced in brick with stone trim. At Temple Sholom Alschuler placed a colonnaded portico without pediment in front of the basilica hall and raised both auditorium and portico on a high basement. The exterior columns articulate the full height of the sanctuary. As the architect explained, "the vertical lines of the columns rising above [the basement] indicate the uplifting purpose of the house of worship."[16] Alschuler's plans, vocabulary of forms, and facing materials provided simple yet dignified formal statements. These became prototypes for designers who were less adept at solving the functional, theoretical, and expressive problems of the synagogue as a building type. Moreover, Alschuler clearly articulated the nature of these problems in local religious publications that likely influenced the stylistic choices of building committees as well as their architects.

## Stone Avenue Temple
**Tucson, Arizona**

Ely Blount

1910



In the same year the Temple Society of Concord was built in Syracuse, a smaller congregation far across the continent also dedicated its new synagogue. This too, was a classical building reflecting many of the aesthetic, political, and religious aspirations of the Syracuse congregation, albeit on a more modest scale.

Temple Emanu-El of Tucson is the oldest synagogue in the Arizona Territory, built several generations after the first Jews arrived in the Arizona territory in the mid-nineteenth century. Built in 1910 after a design by Ely Blount, this building cost only $4,712 to construct (less than 5 percent of the budget for the synagogue built by Syracuse's Temple Society of Concord). Even that money was difficult to raise. The lot was purchased in 1886, but it took twenty-four years to get a building erected.

Though it is small structure consisting of little more than a one-story sanctuary space, the classical articulation of the exterior gives the synagogue dignity, and in early twentieth-century Tucson, it established an acceptable status for the congregation. The brick facade, now painted white, consists of a central bay defined by three large arched windows surmounted by a prominent pediment. This section is matched by twin towers, each with an identical pedimented doorway. Tall twin towers were common on nineteenth-century synagogues, but these are closer in form to Renaissance and Baroque church bell towers. They recall, for example, the prominent bell towers that can be found on area Mission churches such as San Xavier del Bac, just outside Tucson.

There is no full vestibule. The lower spaces of the towers provide tiny transitional spaces between street and sanctuary. The windows on the facade and side illuminate a simple interior, decorated solely with simple ceiling moldings. Many of the windows were filled with simple stained-glass designs, a few of which have survived. A plain rebuilt *bimah* projects into the sanctuary as a slightly raised semicircle.

The synagogue closed in 1949 when the congregation moved to the suburbs, but in recent years the building has been reclaimed and has been restored for public and religious use after serving as home to a radio station and a least fourteen different Christian congregations.

Left: The façade demonstrates that classicism was adopted even in the west. The two towers, however, may recall an older synagogue tradition, or perhaps the influence of local Mission Church architecture.

Above: Since it was first built in 1910 to house Temple Emanu-El, the building has served many Jewish and Christian congregations. It has recently been restored to approximate its original appearance.

Left: The pews are original, but the Ark is lost. The Ark curtain now installed dates from the 1930s.

Right: In the south vestibule is a new wall-high tile mosaic filled with Jewish symbols and appropriate inscriptions. At the top is written "The Torah is a tree of life for those who hold fast to it" (Proverbs. 3:18), a passage recited in the weekly service. Below is written "Let them make me a sanctuary that I may dwell among them" (Exodus 25:8–9). In the center are shown hands making the priestly blessing, flanked by doves. There are also Torah scrolls, menorahs, eternal lamps, and pomegranates. The entire center section is composed of tiles embossed with the Star of David, some including names of donors.

## Congregation Rodef Shalom
## Pittsburgh, Pennsylvania

Palmer & Hornbostel
1907



In opposition to the stolid classicism of Kahn and the archaeologically sensitive work of Brunner is the decorative, even flamboyant synagogue designed by Henry Hornbostel (1867–1961) for Congregation Rodef Shalom in Pittsburgh.[17] Legend has it that Hornbostel beat out Kahn for the commission. True or not, the result was quite new to American synagogue architecture, while still within the tasteful norms of Jewish mercantile-industrial society. Rodef Shalom, built in 1907, has a distinctly Central European flavor, quite distinct from Hornbostel's otherwise mostly classical oeuvre. Architectural historian Franklin Toker has cited the 1883 Budapest train station as a possible source for Hornbostel's design. The design also recalls world's fair pavilions, such as those for the Paris Exposition of 1900, on which Hornbostel worked with his teacher at the Ecole des Beaux Arts, C. L. Girault.[18]

The Reform synagogue is situated at the northwest corner of Fifth and Morewood Avenues in Pittsburgh's fashionable Oakland section, close to several churches, including the 1904 classical First Church of Christ, Scientist located directly across the street and designed by Chicago architect S. S. Beman.[19] It is typical of many "second settlement" synagogues of the period, erected as public buildings around parks and newly designed civic centers for more affluent Jewish populations that had removed themselves from dense urban neighborhoods.

The synagogue is divided into three main parts: the ornate entrance, the sanctuary cube, and the squared dome that surmounts it. The inside reflects similar shapes and motifs, but the decoration is enlivened with applied ornament in the style of Louis Sullivan, and a sensitive use of natural and artificial light. Historian Toker has noted, "Unlike most pre-modern synagogues, there is nothing fake-Moorish here, although the dazzling colors on the terra-cotta bands (now faded) hint so strongly at orientalism that passersby know instinctively that this is not a church."[20]

One of the significant innovations in the design was the introduction of color—both inside and out. The architectural press of the time stated that the work was:

> artistically accomplished as to present an attractive and harmonious effect. The entrance feature and the frieze that encircles the building,

Right: South façade showing dome and large windows into sanctuary.

executed by the Atlantic Terra-Cotta Co., may be regarded as one of the most successful attempts in this direction that has been accomplished in this country. The entire building, with its green dome, buff brick, the polychromatic effect of the terra-cotta, presents an effect highly creditable to the architect and a delightfully restful spot in what would otherwise be a monotonous and uninteresting thoroughfare.[21]

The groined dome of double shell construction is entirely composed of Guastavino tile and has a clear span of 92 feet. The tile is strong enough to replace the steel construction originally intended. The upper, or exposed, shell of the dome is covered with green glazed terra-cotta tiles. Inside, the dome is covered with decorative plaster. At the center is a large octagonal stained-glass skylight.

The sanctuary was designed to seat 1,100 people on the ground floor; with additional seating for 350 in the gallery at the rear. A 20-foot-high oak wainscot runs around the sanctuary wall, above which are large stained-glass memorial windows. The windows, made by the Willett Studio, are unusual, but part of a growing trend at the time of including figural compositions. A large stained-glass window of Moses, for example, was included in the Ark wall of the De Hirsch Synagogue in Seattle, also built in 1907. While all the scenes at Rodef Shalom come from the Hebrew Bible, the artist clearly drew from Christian iconography. "Mercy and Judgment" depicts a bearded man carrying a child and a woman on the ground who represents the despair of poverty. "Moses Interceding for His People" shows Moses praying on a hill, in a manner commonly used in renderings of the contemplative Jesus. In "Ruth and Naomi" two women embrace, similar to church scenes of the meeting of Mary and Elizabeth. A visitor sitting by the bedside of a sick girl and, above, two angels carrying the soul of the deceased in a typically Christian manner is the subject of "Charity."[22] As in many new synagogues of the period, individual, theater-style seats are used, and each rack of seats terminates at the aisle with a pew end or post. The engineering of the synagogue, as well as its religious programming, were up-to-date—it was mechanically ventilated and heated by direct steam system. A Sunday school was placed in a wing to the rear of the main auditorium along with an assembly room, classroom, clubroom, library, and rabbi's study.

Above: Main (west) façade of synagogue with the inscription "My House Shall Be Called a House of Prayer for all People." (Isaiah: 56:7)

Opposite: View of spacious sanctuary looking northwest, showing large octagonal skylight, sanctuary windows, and arched window over main entrance.

IN · LOVING · MEMORY · OF · OUR · PARENTS:
JACOB · AND LENA · KLEE
IN MEMORIAM
JACOB H. CUSKY
EVA CUSKY

Above: The sanctuary looking toward the Ark wall. A large arch enframes the *bimah*, Ark, and organ loft.

Opposite: The large figural stained-glass windows on the north wall of the sanctuary.

Right: A richly decorated freestanding pier—part of the wall that separates the synagogue lot from the street.

# Chapter Four

## Between the Wars: Simpler Forms and Complex Functions (1920s and 1930s)

But I, through your abundant love, enter Your House;
I bow down in awe to your holy temple.

—Psalms 5:8

The 1920s were a decade of radical change in all aspects of American culture, and even staid religious communities were not immune to the allure of the new. From a purely practical view, change was desired within many congregations. As synagogues had gotten larger, the distance from pew to *bimah* seemed longer for many of the congregants. In an age before mechanical amplification, acoustics also suffered in the long boxlike halls.

One solution was the rediscovery of the central plan—a traditional synagogue form common from many different Jewish centers the world over, but relatively unknown in the U.S. until the early twentieth century. As we have seen, during the "Age of Classicism" large, masonry, central-plan synagogues with sanctuaries set beneath grand domes become common in American cities.

In 1890, Temple Beth Zion in Buffalo, New York, was the first American synagogue to fully develop the potential of a central dome, and this was followed by several of the classical structures described in chapter 3. In the 1920s, larger structures, often articulated with variations on Byzantine ornament—such as Temple Emanu-El in San Francisco, designed by Bakewell and Brown; and Temple B'nai Brith, also known as the Wilshire Boulevard Temple in Los Angeles—came to dominate.

William Tachau experimented with several plan types in his many synagogue designs. In 1928, just a year before the stock market crash and the onset of the Great Depression put a halt to all new synagogue construction, he described, somewhat critically, the process that created the more central plan for the synagogue sanctuary.

> Recently a number of plans have been developed in circular, elliptical and polygonal forms, which again owe their inspiration to Byzantine influence. To obtain the imposing effect that such designs require, the dome must be of a lofty character and so pretentious a venture can be only accomplished at great cost; and in many instances such heights result in poor acoustics—a very serious defect in an auditorium.[1]

According to architectural historian Rachel Wischnitzer, "the polygonal single-roofed structure satisfied the desire for clean-cut lines as contrasted with the romantic "disorder" of separately roofed units. However, extensions and annexes, unavoidable in a growing congregation, were found to present a vexing problem in a strictly symmetrical, compact plan."[2]

The Byzantine Revival and the Art Deco synagogues that were popular in the 1920s were primarily studies in spatial geometry. They often emphasized the qualities of the building material (frequently brick and tile), and they tended to limit decoration to flat surface ornament. They emphasized variants on the cube and sphere in their design, and they utilized natural light as much as possible. Lastly, they addressed many modern concerns such as adjustable space, incorporation of multiple functions—including social halls, kitchens, gymnasiums, swimming pools, libraries, schools, and offices—within in a single structure. New to synagogue design considerations in the 1920s was the issue of parking.

Reform and Conservative congregations allowed their members to drive to synagogue on Friday nights and Saturdays, and the location of many of the grand new synagogues required it. The advent of the automobile was altering American urban lifestyles and neighborhood design, and and the car quickly came to influence, albeit subtly, synagogue design, too.

Opposite: The Temple, Atlanta, Georgia. Large sanctuary windows with simple geometric decorations illuminate the sanctuary.

## The Temple–Tifereth Israel
## Cleveland, Ohio

Charles R. Greco
1923



Many of these new considerations of design and use can be seen in Temple Tifereth Israel in Cleveland, one of the most elegant synagogues of the era. Overlooking Cleveland's Rockefeller Park to the east, The Temple, as it is known, served as a gateway to the formerly Jewish neighborhoods that encircled the park. In the interwar period this area was the center of Cleveland's Jewish community, but after World War II, propelled by private automobiles, the community moved to the eastern suburbs. Tifereth Israel has also moved, to a large new campus, but unlike many American congregations it has maintained its old building, too, keeping it as a museum and for use on special occasions.

Congregation Tifereth Israel had been a well-established part of the greater Central–East 55th Street neighborhood when it decided to sell its Central Avenue Synagogue in the early 1920s and relocate to a new site on Ansel Road. The relocation was prompted by the gradual movement of the congregation from the East 55th Street neighborhood to Wade Park and Cleveland Heights. Under the leadership of Rabbi Abba Hillel Silver, the Reform congregation began to build a new synagogue in 1923. The congregation left its older building, a large Richardsonian Romanesque structure by Lehman and Schmitt built in 1894 and reminiscent of Trinity Church in Boston.

Boston architect Charles R. Greco was chosen for the commission, and he created a domed synagogue derived from Byzantine models but nearly stripped of ornamentation. The imposing result is one of the monumental civic structures at University Circle (the area includes Case Western Reserve University and the Cleveland Museum of Art).[3]

Though the site of the new synagogue was impressive, the shape of the lot was not promising. It is an unusually narrow, triangular lot with its narrowest point in the most public position. Greco adopted a polygonal plan for the main body of Congregation Tifereth Israel, allowing the synagogue wings to fan out off the rear sides of the heptagon. The narrowest point of the lot remains empty, providing an impressive approach to the arched entranceway. The sanctuary sits at the point where the lot becomes wide enough, and is entered from its northeast side. Already anticipating what would become the norm for postwar synagogues, there is an ample parking lot to the rear of the building,

Right: View of the sanctuary from the balcony with the Ark wall on left.

and many users of the facilities, which contained many social spaces, naturally enter the complex from the rear.

The earlier synagogue was massive and many faceted, with rusticated stonework, corner towers, and a tall central tower. The new building, however, was sleek and cool, with smooth wall planes, sharp angles, and a monochromatic sheathing in light Indiana limestone. Even today, the Temple looks extremely modern, though its three-arched entry way, its two flanking entrance towers, and its high hemispheric dome still tie it to a historic tradition.

Inside, there is dramatic surface play between the seven prominent ribs that support the main dome and the dome skin. The domed sanctuary is large and all-encompassing, but the dark woods of the balcony and Ark and the lighter block walls create a stark color contrast that boosts the visual excitement. Perhaps it was the poor acoustics at Tifereth Israel that William Tachau had in mind when he wrote of the domed synagogue. The problem was solved, however, with a state-of-the-art amplification system designed to serve the needs of Rabbi Hillel Silver, one of the nation's leading Zionists. "When he spoke," said Israel's first president David Ben-Gurion, "people listened."

Above: The entrance foyer of the Temple is an experience of condensed opulence. Every surface of the space is covered in decoration of fine materials and intricate design. There is a memory of the Moorish style, but it is simplified in the style of the Art Deco. In the gridded ceiling one can see patterns of six-pointed stars, the only explicit Jewish symbolism present.

Opposite: The main approach to the Temple showcases the combination of geometric forms that combine elegance and strength. The design would be imitated by other congregations throughout the country.

Opposite: The sanctuary interior is a vast, high domed space that is intimidating when empty, but unifying when the pews are filled.

Above: The Gries Chapel is decorated with stained-glass windows designed by Arthur Szyk (1894–1951), and in which the names of the twenty-two men of the congregation who died in service in World War II are commemorated, surrounded by Jewish symbols: the Crown of the Law, the harp and diadem of King David, the tablet of the Ten Commandments, and the lion of Judah.

## K.A.M. Isaiah Israel Congregation
**Chicago, Illinois**

Alfred S. Alschuler

1924



In Chicago, the finest example of the domed synagogue was the Byzantine Temple Isaiah dedicated in 1924 and designed by local architect Alfred S. Alschuler (1876–1940).[4] Inspired by the sixth-century Byzantine churches of San Vitale in Ravenna and Hagia Sofia in Istanbul, the octagonal-plan synagogue is topped by a low tile dome. According to the architect, "We have not designed a Byzantine building but have endeavored to produce in concrete, stone, brick and steel, the mental picture developed by the study of this style modified by its contemporary influences and co-ordinated with the proper spirit and functioning of modern Jewish synagogues."[5]

Alschuler maintained, in much the manner of Arnold Brunner, that his style was more truthful to early synagogue architecture than other forms. There is some basis for this claim, as there *were* synagogues throughout the Byzantine empire. Alschuler wrote of how he incorporated motifs of "fragments from an ancient Hebrew Temple recently unearthed in Palestine."[6]

Alschuler was disingenuous, however, as no central-plan synagogues like Temple Isaiah had ever been found. The minaret-like tower next to the main sanctuary masks the facility's tall chimney and is a particularly unusual, albeit picturesque, addition. One critic, obviously unfamiliar with Jewish tradition but full of love for the exotic, wrote:

> It is a beauty and a joy, surrounded by a spacious lawn, trees and a dwelling house environment. Its low, flat dome and horizontal lines are delightfully accentuated by the tall slender chimney, reminiscent of a minaret from which the faint, intoned voice of the musessin would complete the picture of beauty. It is one of those structures that we return to, always eager to get our feel of its beauty of form and color.[7]

Others found the mosque analogy puzzling, and even offensive.[8] But preoccupation with the mosque detracts from the real elegance Alschuler's geometric solution—an octagonal space surmounted by a high dome supported on vaults that spring from eight massive freestanding piers.[9] A semicircular balcony increases the seating that is close to the *bimah* and Ark. The supporting piers are close to the walls to keep the sanc-

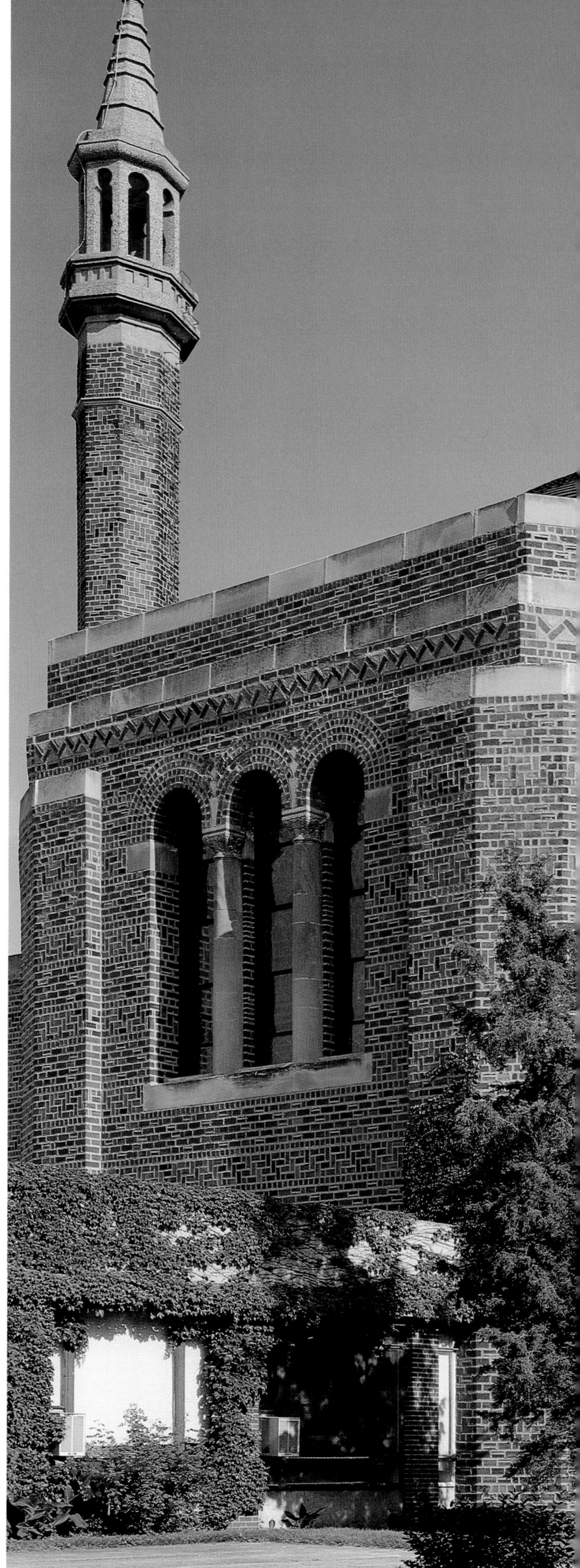

Right: View from the northwest, showing the octagonal form of the sanctuary preceded by lower entry block. On the left rises the smokestack of the heating plant, designed to look like a minaret.

150
YEARS
1847-
1997

tuary space uncluttered. The dome was made of Guastavino tile, like that of Rodef Shalom in Pittsburgh (chapter 3). The tile was both structural and acoustic.[10] The use of Guastavino tiles allows other attractive details, such as the sinuous stairs that twist up to the balcony from either side of the vestibule.

Overall, the building maintains two levels of decoration. The first derives solely from the careful mix of materials and combination of soft earthy colors in the tile and brick. The second is an extensive overlay of explicit Jewish symbols, which crescendo as one progresses through the building. The stylized Decalogue is set over the main entrance, and a more traditional Decalogue sits within the arch above the Ark, designed as a large Syrian arch—a motif from Byzantine Palestine. In the ornate vestibule are emblems of the Twelve Tribes of Israel. The Star of David is prominently depicted throughout the building: in inlaid brick in each of the four great pendentives of the interior vault, in a large roundel at the apex of the dome, in a roundel at the apex of the Ark wall, and above ornate Byzantine capitals.[11] Large freestanding menorahs flank the Ark.

Perhaps the most remarkable decorative element in Temple Isaiah is not architectural. It is a large, figurative stained-glass window representing Moses. This tall image of the prophet holding the tablets of the law is set in the balcony level, and is not easily visible from the sanctuary below. The depiction of figures, even Moses, was unusual in synagogue art, but had appeared in the windows at Rodef Shalom in Pittsburgh (chapter 3) and elsewhere. Moses and his brother Aaron frequently appear in the breastplates that decorate Torah scrolls.

Top: Three arched doorways lead to the entrance foyer. In the tympana above the doors are Jewish symbols: menorah, Star of David and Torah scroll.

Bottom: A winding stairway leading from the entrance foyer to the balcony.

Opposite: Detail of decoration at the balcony level.

Above: Interior of the sanctuary seen from the foyer.

Opposite: View of the balcony, where seating is comfortable. Note the tall stained-glass window depicting Moses.

## Wilshire Boulevard Temple
## Los Angeles, California

Abram M. Edelman, S. Tilden Norton & David C. Allison
1929



The third home of Congregation B'nai B'rith of Los Angeles, commonly known as the Wilshire Boulevard Temple, is more lavish than Temple Isaiah. It is typical of the most monumental and ornate (some would say ostentatious) examples of the domed style. The building was designed by Abram M. Edelman, S. Tilden Norton (honorary president of the Temple) and David C. Allison, and dedicated in 1929.[12]

Edelman, the son of the congregation's first rabbi, had designed the congregation's previous building. Norton was a member of the congregation and had built the first and second homes of Temple Sinai. (The second building, now the Korean Philadelphia Presbyterian Church, was in the mid-Wilshire area and was erected in 1926. It was considered the home of Conservative Judaism in the Los Angeles area.)

B'nai B'rith traces its origins to the first Jewish worship service in Los Angeles, held in 1851. Long in the shadow of the much more prosperous San Francisco community, Los Angeles Jews managed to erect an impressive brick Gothic synagogue in 1873, and then to replace this with the building further "uptown" in 1896 designed by Edelman. The latter was a two-towered structure combining Romanesque and Moorish motifs owing much to urban synagogues of the previous generation. Only a year separated it from Arnold Brunner's Shearith Israel in New York, and less than decade from Albert Kahn's Beth El in Detroit and other classical synagogues. The building was old-fashioned within a few years of its completion.

The new Wilshire Temple was the dream of Rabbi Edgar Magnin who, over a career of several decades, forged a Jewish identity for Los Angeles that joined pioneers and Hollywood moguls. Magnin came to B'nai B'rith as assistant rabbi in 1915 and from that time on he championed a new synagogue building. The involvement of the Hollywood moviemakers after World War I and Magnin's promotion to senior rabbi in 1919 allowed the building to go forward. Mostly displaced New Yorkers with marginal religious interest, the Hollywood producers were attracted to the media-savvy Magnin's image of a popular modern Judaism.[13] Like Rabbi Silver in Cleveland, Magnin used the platform of the new synagogue to reach a national audience.

Rabbi Magnin also foresaw the movement of the city, and especially its Jewish population, westward. In this, the Wilshire Boulevard

Left: Interior of the sanctuary, looking toward the Ark wall. Note Hugo Ballin's painted frieze that encircles the space. It depicts Jewish history.

This page: Main façade on Wilshire Boulevard.
Opposite: The huge drum of the Temple seen from the intersection go Wilshire Boulevard and S. Hobart Boulevard.



Temple was both typical and prescient in anticipating the increased suburbanization of American Jewish life. Because the new synagogue was beyond the "car line," it presaged L.A.'s near-total dependence on the automobile, an urban-suburban transformation that would affect most Jewish communities only after World War II.

From the street, the Wilshire Boulevard Temple appears massive with an enormous dome towering over an important Los Angeles intersection, at Wilshire and South Hobart Boulevard (though at the time of its construction the site was a sparsely settled residential area beyond the city's western limit). The Wilshire Boulevard facade (on the building's south side) includes a monumental Romanesque-style three-arch portal that serves as a porch to what seems, from street level, to be a traditional Romanesque nave with large rose window and sloping roofs. But this nave is extremely shallow, covering only a vestibule that serves as an entryway into a vast octagonal sanctuary.

A simpler variation of the Wilshire Boulevard facade is repeated on the west, but the full height of the octagonal drum and circular dome is visible from the corner of the building. Behind the Temple a substantial facility was built to meet most of the needs then considered essential in a synagogue center.

The Wilshire arrangement of three arched openings, shallow vestibule, and domed sanctuary is similar to Temple Isaiah in Chicago, but the overall massing more closely resembles Temple Emanu-El in San Francisco. Wilshire's congregation was certainly competing with Emanu-El, designed by Arthur Brown, Jr., John Bakewell, Jr., and Sylvain Schnaittacher and built in 1926. The San Francisco Reform temple offers a more eclectic variation of the Byzantine model. Its large domed sanctuary is a mix of Byzantine and Romanesque styles, with the *bimah* capped by a ciborium that resembles early medieval Italian examples (but the Romanesque Revival Fassanenstrasse Synagogue in Berlin employed a similar design). The synagogue presents a more pronounced Mediterranean look, however, with its stucco exterior walls. Four large bronze chandeliers hang from the dome.[14] Temple Emanu-El was well illustrated in an article by William Tachau in September 1928 just as the Wilshire Boulevard Temple was being built.[15]

The sanctuary at Wilshire is overwhelming. The 100-foot dome creates a spectacular space rich in colors, texture, and materials. Black Belgian marble columns, teak doors, gold Ark fixtures, and bronze chandeliers combine to create a shimmering world closed off from everyday concerns. Despite the avowedly modern and Reform position of the rabbi and the congregation, the enormous Ark contains some traditional elements, such as the depiction of the blessing hands of the high priests.

The Wilshire Boulevard Temple is also important because it reintroduced narrative, figurative art into the sanctuary, in the form of a long, painted history of the Jewish people by Hugo Ballin that encircles the prayer hall. While the influence of this innovation was not felt immediately because of the onset of the Great Depression just months after the synagogue's dedication, it did initiate changes in Jewish attitudes toward synagogue art that emerged after World War II.[16] Rabbi Magnin wrote:

> The day is over when liberal-minded people are likely to worship images and painting, and so we decided to place them on the walls of our Wilshire Boulevard Temple in such a manner as not to conflict in any way with the Jewish spirit, but rather to revive it. The Synagogue, particularly the Reform temple, is generally too cold in its architectural treatment. We need more warmth and mysticism. In addition to this the portrayal of our history in figurative form stimulates the imagination and a curiosity for deeper knowledge about our own traditions.

WILSHIRE
3663

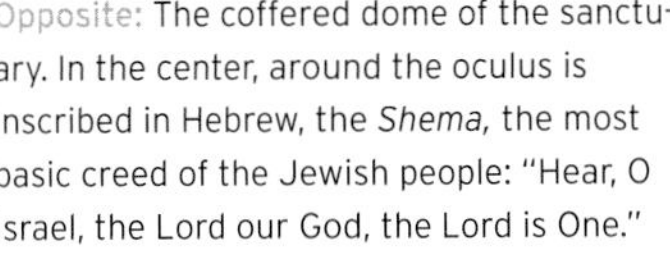

Opposite: The coffered dome of the sanctuary. In the center, around the oculus is inscribed in Hebrew, the *Shema,* the most basic creed of the Jewish people: "Hear, O Israel, the Lord our God, the Lord is One."

Above: A view across the sanctuary to the western lunette, which depicts the Messianic Age based on passages from the Books of Isaiah and Micah.

Top right: The vestibule before the sanctuary recalls contemporary lobbies of movie palaces.

Bottom right: View into the vibrantly colored sanctuary.

No doubt this recognition of a validity of visual culture appealed to Hollywood Jews, since they made their living creating a new American business and art devoted to visual storytelling. Rabbi Magnin continued: "In an age in which people desire visualizations as evidenced by motion pictures, television and the increasing use of illustrations in newspapers and magazines, the synagogue may also bring a better message to its people by falling in line with this trend."[17]

Not surprisingly, the three Warner brothers and their wives, in memory of two deceased brothers, sponsored the innovative synagogue decorations. Significantly, Warner Brothers Studio's biggest hit to date was the talking sensation *The Jazz Singer*, which featured scenes shot in the Orthodox Breed Street Shul (Congregation Talmud Torah) built in 1923, also by A.M. Edelman (with Leo Barnett). The money made from that film allowed Warner Brothers Studios to move in 1928 from Sunset Boulevard to the 110-acre Burbank lot that has been its home ever since. Significantly, just as the movie documented Al Jolsen's transcendence of his Orthodox roots, the Warner brothers preferred for themselves a synagogue experience radically different from Congregation Talmud Torah on Boyle Heights.

Hugo Ballin (1879–1956) was an admired artist who had painted the decorations in the State Capitol building in Madison, Wisconsin, in 1912, before moving to Hollywood where he became a prolific and accomplished film artist and designer. After painting the murals in the Wilshire Boulevard Temple, he created murals in the Griffith Park observatory and the Los Angeles Times Building (1934).[18]

* * *

The Byzantine Revival style was especially common for synagogues after World War I, and by the 1920s Chicago's large Jewish community had wholeheartedly embraced the style. Several new synagogues with central plans inspired by Temple Isaiah, or with basilica-plans adorned with Byzantine-inspired ornament were built during the decade. A similar trend can be seen in New York City, with a series of major new Byzantine-style synagogues erected in Manhattan and Brooklyn throughout the decade of financial boom.

While the central dome over the sanctuary space became especially common, a frequent urban variation of this style emphasized a single giant facade portal, as at B'nai Jeshurun (1918), Park Avenue Synagogue, Unity Synagogue (later Mount Neboh), and Temple Emanu-El (1929), all in Manhattan.

Shortly after World War I decorative motifs appeared in synagogues that share many of the characteristics that became common in the 1920s as part of the Art Deco style. In the Jewish context, the sources for these designs are varied, but many clearly derive from the nineteenth-century taste for Moorish decoration, which favored geometric patterning and complex linear motifs.

Because of the popularity of adapting these Moorish-inspired elements to Byzantine-style buildings, American Jewish communities were quicker than other religious groups to embrace some Art Deco forms and decorative schemes, as well as other variants of modernism.

**Wilshire Boulevard Temple** Los Angeles, California

But because few synagogues were built in the 1930s, the potential evolution from Byzantine to Deco to Art Moderne never was fully developed. A hint of the possibilities can be seen in Temple Beth El in Miami Beach, designed by Charles R. Greco in the 1940s, which fits into the city's general Art Moderne trend that flourished before World War II.

The 1920s also witnessed a revival of Near Eastern forms as a legitimate Jewish style predating Moorish and Byzantine prototypes—indeed, harking all the way back to Solomon's Temple. Temple Israel on Commonwealth Avenue in Boston (1906) is an early example of this style, while Philadelphia's Rodeph Shalom designed by Simon and Simon, which in 1927 replaced a Moorish style building designed by Frank Furness in 1870, is a late version. On the outside, Rodeph Shalom's massive structure resembles Cecil B. DeMille's version of Babylon as much as it recalls specific archaeological sources. Inside, however, Rodeph Shalom is historicist—modeled in large part on the Synagogue in Florence, Italy.[19]

That Hollywood should provide models for synagogues is not as strange as it seems. First, many architects of synagogues, such as S. Tilden Norton, were also designing lavish movie palaces of the sort that were springing up across the country. It was the movie palace that inherited the Moorish style that had been prevalent in synagogues in the late nineteenth century.[20] Beginning with synagogues such as Alschuler's classical Sinai Temple, the auditorium model was increasingly adopted for synagogues.

Opposite: Stairway to the balcony.
Above: Detail of sanctuary mural by Hugo Ballin. This scene depicts Moses, the tablets of the Law, Joshua and his soldiers, and Samson.

## Congregation Emanu-El of the City of New York

New York, New York

Robert B. Kohn, Charles Butler & Clarence S. Stein

1930

One of the last and largest full expressions of architectural optimism and opulence in American synagogue building before the Depression and World War II was the enormous Congregation Emanu-El on Fifth Avenue at 65th Street in New York. This building, touted as the largest synagogue in the world, is the fifth home of the Reform congregation that began in 1845 in a private home on the Lower East Side. From its start, the architectural aspirations of the congregation were high. In 1847 the congregation purchased its first building, a former church on Chrystie Street, which was then remodeled by Leopold Eidlitz. In 1862 they erected an imposing new building at Fifth Avenue and 43rd Street, which the *New York Times* described at the time of its dedication the "architectural sensation of the city."[21]

The size and cost of the 1920s undertaking, as well as its location in the capital of finance and communications, would, under normal circumstances, have guaranteed tremendous influence for this massive structure and for its prominent congregation. History, however, largely deprived the building such prestige—it was dedicated on January 10, 1930, just a few months after the terrible crash of the stock market.

As Robert Stern has pointed out, "In the course of the move [to the new site] three New York landmarks were lost: the old synagogue by Leopold Eidlitz of 1868, a vivid combination of Viollet-le-Duc's structural theories and Saracenic ornament; Brunner & Tryon's building of 1892 for Temple Beth-El, whose congregation merged with that of Emanu-El in 1927; and at the new site, Richard Morris Hunt's 1891–95 French chateau for John Jacob Astor IV."[22]

The synagogue was designed by Robert B. Kohn, Charles Butler, and Clarence S. Stein. The architects first considered a domed structure similar in shape to the big Reform synagogues in Los Angeles, San Francisco, and other cities.[23] In the end, a basilica plan opening onto Fifth Avenue was adopted, in keeping with the arrangements of the earlier synagogues that merged congregations—Temple Emanu-El and Beth El.

Beth El had given up its prominent synagogue at Fifth Avenue and 76th Street, an enormous building designed by Arnold Brunner before his discovery of classicism. The great dome of Beth El had been a landmark on upper Fifth Avenue for many years. The new synagogue, like the older ones, was oriented with its Ark against the east wall and its

Right: The front of the synagogue is a massive portal onto New York's most fashionable street.

UNNECESSARY
NOISE
PROHIBITED
ONE WAY
F.D.R.
DRIVE

facade receiving the full afternoon light from Central Park (something the sanctuary still enjoys despite the construction of more and more high-rise buildings on the park's western side). A Temple house was erected behind the sanctuary, entered from 65th Street. The large Beth El chapel was built adjacent to the sanctuary immediately to the north.

The facade of Tempel Emanu-El conveys what will be seen inside, though, despite the exterior height, the viewer is inevitably surprised by the enormity of the space within. The facade is organized as a colossal gabled front, with a single huge, slightly recessed arch enclosing windows and doorways, and braced by stair towers on either side, which read as solid masonry buttresses. The exterior massing of the synagogue is close to many fine urban churches of the period designed by Bertram Grosvenor Goodhue, with whom Stein had worked in the past and who was a consultant on this project. The facade recalls several other Manhattan synagogues built in the period, notably B'nai Jeshurun (Walter S. Schneider and Henry Beaumont Herts, 1918), the Park Avenue Synagogue (Deutsch & Schneider, 1926), and the now destroyed Mount Neboh Synagogue formerly on West 79th Street (Walter S. Schneider, 1927–28).

Entry is through three fairly low rectangular openings set beneath four tall lancet windows that are separated by elongated colonettes and topped with small arches with vaguely Byzantine decorative motifs. Above this composition is a large rose window. Surmounting the arch, in a stepped pattern, are seven more narrow windows defined by applied Romanesque colonettes and topped by elongated arches. While the composition does not copy any specific historic building, the style is fully suggestive of medieval churches. From Central Park and the street this impression is augmented by the visibility of a campanile-like tower over the eight-story Temple house. While such towers are not unknown in American synagogue design, they had become fairly rare in the previous half century, since the erection of a tall single Gothic spire at the synagogue in Savannah, Georgia, in 1876. Just as the "minaret" at the Isaiah Temple in Chicago conceals a smokestack, here the apparent bell tower hides the water tanks and elevator machinery.

The interior of Temple Emanu-El is enormous, a rectangular hall 103 feet high, 150 feet long, and 77 feet wide. The sanctuary seats 2,500 people. Wall decoration is minimal, and the nave is defined by a series of huge round-headed arches that run the length of the sanctuary. These are ultimately echoed in an even bigger arch defining the eastern Ark wall, which encloses the Ark as well as the choir and organ lofts above it. The size and rhythm of the interior recall other New York synagogues, especially the recent buildings in which Walter Schneider had a hand, and recent Gothic churches, such as those by Bertram Goodhue (Holy Trinity) and Ralph Adams Cram (St. John the Divine). But the interior of Temple Emanu-El stands apart from these through its use of round arches and thick, mostly unadorned supporting piers. While there is some recollection of the lofty powerful spaces of medieval Lombard churches, the only contemporary buildings that really compete in spaciousness with the synagogue are contemporary secular halls—especially train stations such as New York's Grand Central Terminal (1903–1913).

Architect Clarence E. Stein wrote, "We felt ourselves free in choice of detail with which to ornament the structural form," and the architects

Above: View of the entrance vestibule, offering a transitional space between the busy street and the hush of the sanctuary.

Opposite: A full view of the East (Ark) wall from the rear balcony. The rhythm of the large arches on either side lead the viewer's gaze to the great arch over the Ark.

Opposite: Interior, looking back towards entrance (west) wall.

Left: Facing Central Park, the large west windows capture a lot of light, and they need to since the interior of the synagogue is so vast.

Right: Detail of the sanctuary interior showing the side arches, stained glass clerestory windows, and decorated ceiling construction.

developed the design "from the Romanesque as used in the south of Italy under the influence of the Moorish, because it was an expression of the intermingling of Occidental and Oriental thought. We might just as well have started with some other style, as the detail gradually developed into new forms and certainly new scale in the drafting room and in the sculptor's studio. Above all it was scale that governed our form."[24]

Shallow aisles along the sides shelter low galleries supported by marble columns. These galleries are almost vestigial. Since this is a Reform synagogue with mixed seating, they exist for overflow seating on the High Holidays. The balconies importantly provide infill for the enormous bays of the nave. Unlike in cathedrals where chapels and altars can be set within large arched bays, there is really no use for such spaces in a synagogue.

Above left: Detail of the pulpit, built onto the left side of the *bimah*.
Above right: Ark.
Opposite: Detail of the decorative frame surrounding the Ark.

Structurally, the walls are actually self-supporting, while the exterior flying buttresses are structural steel covered with stone. The treatment of the ceiling departs from the fifty-year tradition of vaults. Here, the ceiling appears to be an open timber roof reminiscent of early Christian basilicas, but the walnut is supported by steel trusses covered with plaster. Rich materials including Siena travertine are used throughout the building.

An abbreviated version of the Ten Commandments is on the Ark's bronze grille. Seven-branched menorahs flank the Ark. The Star of David is repeated in the mosaics and windows of the temple, and the lion of Judah and the Royal Crown of the Torah are also represented.

A pamphlet published during the time of its construction described the style of the building as an "adaptation of a very early Romanesque, as it was used in Syria and in the East and found occasionally in Sicily, influence by Eastern and Arab invasions."[25] This description alone suggests the underlying eclecticism of the design, while identifying its strong medievalizing elements.

Immediately to the north of the sanctuary is the Beth El Chapel, which is only two bays long and seats 350. Symbols of the Twelve Tribes of Israel decorate the Fifth Avenue facade, and over the door is a verse from the Book of Exodus (28:17): "This is none other than the house of God." The inscription on the exterior frieze of the chapel is from Isaiah (32:17): "And the work of righteousness, quietness and security forever." But the main access to the chapel is directly through the front two north bays of the main sanctuary. The two domes of the chapel are supported by six columns of pink Westerly granite while the side walls rest on arches springing from marble columns. Verdello marble is used for the wainscots and for the sidewalls.

* * *

Classicism had, for the most part, run its creative course by the end of World War I when new architectural forms took the lead in architectural innovation. But through the 1920s the style was still preferred in official circles, and Washington was in the midst of dressing itself in a classical mantle of white temple-like buildings. Henry Bacon's design for the (then unbuilt) Lincoln Memorial was adapted by his friend Albert Kahn for his second Temple Beth El building (1927) in Detroit. Kahn's building resembles his Angell Hall at the University of Michigan (1922), also inspired by Bacon's design.

In New York, Chicago, and elsewhere, classical synagogues of various types continued to be built into the 1920s. In New York, Congregation Shaare Zedek began a new classical building on West 93rd Street in 1921, which was dedicated in 1923. The design by architects Sommerfeld & Steckler is well suited to the narrow side street site. The four-story facade is treated as a giant temple front with a pediment set upon Corinthian pilasters.[26]

Classicism continued to thrive in tandem with the newer Byzantine-inspired variations. Chicago's large Kehilath Anshe Maariv, designed by Newhouse and Bernham, was built in 1924, the same year as Temple Isaiah. An eight-column Ionic portico spans the building's entire width. Inside, seating divides the wide hall into three sections. Corinthian columns near the walls supported the ceiling, the middle section of which was a shallow vault, and Corinthian pilasters decorated a concave Ark wall. The Ark itself, a small wooden cabinet, appeared quite modest against the pilasters. The organ was visible in two bays on either side of Ark wall and *bimah*.

Congregation Emanu-El of the City of New York New York, New York

## The Temple
## Atlanta, Georgia
Philip Trammel Shutze
1931

One of the last great classical designs is that of the Temple in Atlanta, home of the Hebrew Benevolent Society—Atlanta's oldest Jewish congregation. Designed by Philip Trammel Shutze (1890–1982) and dedicated in 1931, the building is now widely known for being bombed in 1958 during the civil rights movement because its rabbi, Jacob Rothschild, was an active supporter of Martin Luther King.[27]

Shutze was a leading classical architect of the twentieth century and continued building Italian-inspired villas and palatial homes as well as government and civic buildings even after World War II. He studied at Columbia University, where he would have been intimately familiar with the Roman classicism of Charles McKim. His 1915 dissertation was a design for a gymnasium modeled on the Forum of Trajan in Rome. His subsequent three-year stay in Rome as a fellow at the American Academy in Rome furthered his lifelong commitment to classical architecture. Like Albert Kahn, Shutze was greatly influenced by the Pantheon, which he helped measure with other students from the Academy in 1917.[28]

After Shutze was hired by Rabbi David Marx to design a new building for the Hebrew Benevolent Society, his first design drew more on Venetian models than on Roman, combining Renaissance elements from Palladian churches, Baroque massing, and a dome that recalled Baldassare Longhena's Santa Maria delle Salute. This design was rejected because of cost, but perhaps also because it closely resembled a Catholic church. There is no indication that Schutze was familiar with Venetian synagogues, or that the congregation knew that the seventeenth-century Scuola Levantina, one of Venice's grandest synagogues, was probably designed by Longhena's workshop.

A new design was more austere, and closer to Shutze's Roman roots. It was also more in keeping with the classical tradition in American architecture familiar in the south through the historic Beth Elohim synagogue in Charleston. The result is a composite building. It is elegant but hardly original, except in its unexpected combination of classical building parts that normally would be strangers to each other.

The facade consists of two temple forms—a round temple atop a square one. The round form contains a domed lantern. The main facade is designed as a classical temple front whose doorway is adapted from

Right: Philip Trammel Shutze's classical design for the Temple combines two ancient prototypes, one on top of the other.

THE TEMPLE
כי ביתי בית־תפלה
יקרא לכל־העמים

Opposite: The finely proportioned and detailed façade is a composition using simple geometry—squares, circles and triangles. A Baroque-style doorway is subtly inserted into an Ionic colonnade.

Below: The unusual Ark is designed to look like a movable golden chest, recalling perhaps the Ark of the Covenant. It is in fact permanent, and is set on a second level above the *bimah*.

Right: Detail of the rich stucco decoration of the pendentives that support the saucer dome, the arches that span deep niches on each side, and the frieze that runs along the top of all the sanctuary walls.

Gian Lorenzo Bernini's small church of Sant'Andrea al Quirnale in Rome. It consists of a screen of four Ionic columns supporting a pediment. The central bay is articulated with a protruding semi-circular porch supported on four smaller Tuscan Doric columns. As in Bernini's church, the porch roof exactly equals the size of the tympanum (window above the door), and it appears cut out and folded down. Set on this roof against the window is a sculpted Decalogue set within a large scallop shell, indicating that this is a synagogue, not a church. The semicircular porch frieze is decorated with Jewish symbols.

The interior and exterior contain classical details adapted to synagogue use by the incorporation of Hebrew references. Rabbi Marx was involved in these designs. The decorative program of the Ark and *bimah* includes two bronze griffins and candelabra that surround the railing, detailed with triple laurel wreaths flanked by swirling ribbons. The gold-leafed Ark, modeled loosely on biblical descriptions of the Ark of the Covenant, was placed within a dramatic semicircular space with four Ionic columns supporting a curving beam. Behind the brown *scagliola* columns (painted by Athos Menaboni), golden curtains suggest the tent fabric that surrounded the ancient tabernacle. Above the Ark is the eternal light suspended from the eagle and stars in the Great Seal of the United States, a sign that the light of Israel in this country is dependent on the founding principles of the United States. The synagogue faces a grass lawn but the original design called for a staircase of narrowing width as one approached from the street, a device Shutze used in some of his villa projects. This perspectival illusion would have further dramatized the facade.

### Synagogue Centers: More than a Sanctuary

As part of the building boom of the 1920s that saw such impressive synagogues rising across America, the activities that took place within and around the synagogue expanded. As suggested by the program of the Pittsburgh Platform of 1885, the synagogue needed to reach out to the secular world to help draw Jews to its religious activities. When the Conservative movement was begun, the idea of a Jewish Center caught on even more, especially due to the efforts of Mordecai Kaplan (1881–1983). Kaplan organized the Jewish Center in New York and later founded the Reconstructionist movement, which defines Judaism as an "evolving religious civilization" with secular cultural elements essential to spirituality.

Sports, education, and entertainment were used to entice less observant Jews in to the synagogue, and during this period the new Jewish Center strove to duplicate and thus replace many secular institutions. In 1916 Kaplan articulated his vision for the synagogue center:

> The function of the Synagogue will appear in a new light. . . . It should become a social center where the Jews of the neighborhood may find every possible opportunity to give expression to their social and play instincts. It must become the Jew's second home. It must become his club, his theatre and his forum.[29]

The goal was to create an alternate Jewish world in which all Jews could sample a full array of social options. Architect William Tachau wrote: "The idea sprang from a desire to widen the scope of religious influence and to awaken the interest of the younger members of the community to their religious and social obligations. These buildings are usually placed in conjunction with the Sabbath school, so that that the classrooms during the weekdays can be used for various social activities."[30]

The central element of these social centers was the auditorium, which served as an assembly room for the religious school. Some synagogues built these halls with fixed seating and a permanent stage for theatricals and movies, but most erected open, flexible spaces that could be used for all sorts of events, especially receptions, lunches, dinners, and other festive occasions. A social hall at Temple Society of Concord (chapter 3) was added to the 1910 synagogue in 1928 and is a good example of this type of multipurpose room. Significantly this room, and others like it at synagogues across the country, remained a space apartfully defined. In the postwar years, social halls would be laid out in closer relation to the main sanctuary so the spaces could be joined. Full kitchens often complement these social halls, and in some Conservative and all Orthodox synagogues there must be two kitchens to maintain the laws of kashrut.

Many synagogues also had gymnasiums and sometimes even swimming pools—usually in the basement under the sanctuary or under the social hall. Rooms were also "required for women's activities, in which girls' clubs can meet and where classes in sewing, cooking, and the domestic arts find adequate space and comfort . . . boys' club rooms are also included in the scheme and a swimming pool and bowling alley are part of the programme," according to Tachau.[31] Most of these large complexes were created in the economic boom years of the 1920s. With the coming of hard times, many hardly functioned before they were forced to close. Changing demographics and Jewish settlement patterns meant that many of these expensive centers were not revived when times got better, but were sold for non-Jewish use. A new form of synagogue center was to evolve in the suburbs.

Opposite: The Temple, Atlanta, Georgia. Sanctuary interior looking toward the entrance wall and balcony. The simple form of the benches recalls those of early 19th-century synagogues and churches.

# Chapter Five

## Towards a New Architecture: The Modern Synagogue (1945–1955)

How fair are your tents, O Jacob,
your dwellings, O Israel.

—Numbers 24:5

An article about synagogue design in the November 1939 issue of *Architectural Record* was prophetic in its last lines, "A still further step in synagogue design will be attained when the architect . . . is able to use as his means of expression the essential architectural qualities of the structure and free himself entirely of literary and stylistic decoration."[1] Still, in the 1940s, it was not clear which way synagogue design would go.

Beginning in 1944, Rabbi William G. Braude of Temple Beth-El in Providence, Rhode Island, corresponded with representatives of both the "old guard" of synagogue designers (including Charles Greco, a practitioner of the Art Deco and Byzantine styles) and modernists Eric Mendelsohn and Percival Goodman.[2] The taste for historical styles varied by region. In New England congregations preferred vapid Colonial Revival knock-off designs as more fitting to their environment. In 1949, at Temple Emanu-El in Worcester, Massachusetts, Greco deviated from his earlier Byzantine-style work to create a synagogue that looks more like a Congregationalist church, complete with spire. Greco's design recalls an earlier Temple Emanu-El built in 1929 in Greensboro, North Carolina, by Hobart B. Upjohn.[3] Temple Israel of Hollywood, California, commissioned Samuel E. Lunden and S. Charles Lee in 1945 to design a new synagogue adapting the popular California Mission style.[4]

Some of the planning aspects of prewar Jewish centers, which allowed expansion of the sanctuary and the multiple use of spaces, dictated a more modern aesthetic. First seen in the synagogues of Albert Kahn, these new elements were fully developed by Eric Mendelsohn at B'nai Amoona in St. Louis and the Park Synagogue in Cleveland, and in the early synagogues of Percival Goodman at Millburn, New Jersey, Springfield, Massachusetts, and Providence, Rhode Island, in the 1940s and 1950s. These features subsequently become standard in newer religious buildings of all sorts. Beginning with Frank Lloyd Wright's Beth Sholom Synagogue in Elkins Park, Pennsylvania, synagogue congregations and architects rejected ties to history through stylistic allusions. Instead, they manipulated form for symbolic association, frequently favoring building profiles that recalled tents or mountains. Exceptions to this trend are the many buildings that refer in plan, elevation, detail, or material to the wooden synagogues of Poland, made known in this country in publications especially since the 1950s.[5]

Like many of the new Reform and Conservative synagogues of the interwar period, postwar suburban synagogues were also designed as synagogue centers. These facilities offered programs to strengthen Jewish identity and augment Jewish education.

Though new synagogues in the suburbs were designed to serve a variety of needs formerly met by cohesive, essentially homogenous urban neighborhoods, within a fairly short time Jewish community centers (JCCs) that reached across congregational lines were also established. Synagogues gave special attention to school facilities as bastions against the inevitable assimilation of postwar suburban life, and these became prominent elements in new synagogue design. Separate community centers offered a greater mix of secular and religious activities—sometimes competing with individual synagogue offerings, but more often relieving synagogues of the cost of operating separate facilities. As early as the 1920 some rabbis were lamenting that the cost of these expanded services was not only financial, but also spiritual. Rabbis had to serve as social directors as well as religious and spiritual teachers and guides.

Opposite: Congregation Kneses Tifereth Israel, Port Chester, New York. Philip Johnson's design combines many of the elements that become commonplace in post–World War II synagogues—stark geometric forms, bold color contrasts, and exposed construction details.

ברוכים הבאים בשם יהוה

## Eric Mendelsohn

Eric Mendelsohn (1887–1953) practiced architecture in Germany, Holland, England, and Palestine before arriving in the United States in 1942. His architecture reflects many different styles. He was an impatient man—a trait that can be seen in the directness and fluidity of his drawings, and in the career trajectory that led him through many distinct phases in several countries. Still, through it all he was an expressive modernist with a love of concrete and glass.

Mendelsohn's last designs for six American synagogues were intended to excite worshipers' imaginations and to seduce their minds into contemplation. The sanctuaries of these synagogue centers are characterized by elegant curves unadorned with decoration.[6] When Mendelsohn died in 1953 at age sixty-six, only two of this series of large synagogues and community centers were completed. The others were completed after his death. As a group, they had revived both his career and his creative energies. They indelibly put his stamp on the half-century of synagogue design in the U.S. and abroad that was to follow. In 1946, before any of his new designs had been created, Mendelsohn, a Jew, had written about synagogues:

> This period demands centers of worship where the spirit of the Bible is not an ancient mirage, but a living truth, where Jehovah is not a desert King, but our Guide and Companion. It demands temples that will bear witness of man's material achievements and, at the same time, symbolize our spiritual renascence. A question no architect can pass upon, but the answer will inevitably be recorded in the pages of history now being written.[7]

Spreading this message, Mendelsohn began to receive synagogue commissions in the mid-1940s, first with B'nai Amoona in St. Louis in 1945. The postwar rise of suburbs had accelerated the dispersal of younger families of all religions, including Jews, and spawned much new synagogue construction. Mendelsohn, with Jewish credentials and an established reputation, was sought out by progressive synagogues. These congregations were eager to break with the historicism of the past—especially in light of the horrors of the Holocaust—and placed a high value on Mendelsohn's international stature as a modernist. An exhibition of Mendelsohn's work had traveled to St. Louis during 1944.

It was Mendelsohn's architectural mission from 1946 until his untimely death to create an expressive language in which to develop a very practical Jewish communal arrangement for the modern age. During this time he articulated specific needs for the new synagogue center:

> Thus our temples should reject the anachronistic representation of God as a feudal lord, should apply contemporary building styles and architectural conceptions to make God's house a part of the democratic community in which he dwells. Temples should reject in their interiors the mystifying darkness of an illiterate time and should place their faith in the light of day. The House of God should either be an inspiring place for festive occasions that lift up the heart of man, or an animated gathering place for a fellowship warming men's thoughts and intentions by the fire of the divine word given forth from altar and pulpit right in their midst.[8]

In the mid-1940s Mendelsohn created hundreds of dynamic sketches for synagogues, which would come to comprise one of the most powerful series of modern architectural drawings of the twentieth century.[9] Drawn with broad pencil strokes, Mendelsohn's first drawings for B'nai Amoona resemble a submarine emerging from water. The drawings show the sanctuary developing from a cylindrical form to its eventual rectangular shape. In the building itself the expressive energy is provided by a sweeping parabolic concrete roof supported on massive curved steel beams. The rest of the building is constructed of concrete blocks with brick surfaces.

Mendelsohn presented his first concept for B'nai Amoona in February 1946, and this evolved throughout the year.[10] Early on Mendelsohn arrived at the plan arrangement for the various parts of the complex, balancing the sanctuary with administrative and education buildings around a central courtyard, though the articulation of the individual elements took time to resolve. Construction finally began in September 1948. The use of a parabolic roof derived from Mendelsohn's earliest work. Elements in all of his synagogue designs recall such early German projects as the famed Einstein Tower in Potsdam more than his later, more rationalist office buildings, hospitals, and other large commissions.

Opposite: Entrance to Park Synagogue, Cleveland, Ohio. The inscription over the doorway declares, "Blessed are those that come in the name of the LORD."

## Park Synagogue
## Cleveland, Ohio

Eric Mendelsohn
1953



In June 1946 Mendelsohn began work on Park Synagogue, for the Conservative Congregation in Cleveland. The topography of the site—thirty acres of woodland, set on a ridge overlooking Euclid Avenue—gave Mendelsohn more freedom than the urban environment in St. Louis and helped shape the project into a long, low building that rises out of the undulating land. From a distance the massive dome is a landscape feature as well as an architectural marker.

Rabbi Armand Cohen remembered that on the day Mendelsohn was in Cleveland to interview for the job, he already had a drawing of "the outlines of the Park Synagogue, virtually as it stands today."[11] He created an axial design as the core of a complex that was expected to grow over the years. Through this solution Mendelsohn made sure further development of the school and community facilities would not overshadow the sanctuary. In February 1949 the final design was ready, and in May 1953 the building was dedicated.

The complex is laid out as a long wedge, with offices and classrooms in structures that now surround a trapezoidal patio behind a dominating dome. The distribution of parts is not unlike the earlier B'nai Amoona—but here strung out along a central axis rather than tightly held together in an enclosed square.

At the tip of the wedge, projecting like the bow of a ship, is a small daily chapel. Though a strong design element and an attractive space, it is entirely overshadowed by the immense dome of the main sanctuary. The visual weight of the dome counters the dynamic horizontal thrust of the building's base. Inside, the sanctuary is striking because of its enormity and because the dome seems to float down to engulf the congregants, rather than to soar away from them. The dome's base is at the height of the seating area, thrusting the worshipers into domed space. Previously in church and synagogue architecture, domes were an ethereal area into which only the eyes could wander, but Mendelsohn put the congregants at the intersection of earthly and heavenly space. The massive *bimah* cuts into the hemisphere of the dome in an act of expressive architectural integration that recalls Gian Lorenzo Bernini's breaking of the dome molding in the Roman Baroque church of Sant' Andrea al Qurinale in Rome—a Baroque predecessor to Mendelsohn's design.

Right: The large Ark unites the spaces two realms, one of mundane individual seating, and one of unified celestial space.

Mendelsohn was a master of light—with which he flooded the interior to great effect. The dome's base, or drum, is made of glass that extends into glass-lined ambulatories. The light that filters through the glass drum makes the concrete dome appear to levitate.

The low dome symbolizes the closeness of heaven and earth, and increases the intimacy of the large building. Mendelsohn said on this subject: "Thank God, the building rises with the contour of the land and doesn't shake its fist at God." The dome is a symbol of formal purity, unity, and universality. It makes the interior "a single, undivided room in which everyone can hear and see easily . . . and have a sense of congregational unity."[12]

The Park Synagogue sanctuary is one of the earliest—and best—uses of the device known as the "flexible plan," which connects two spaces for increased seating capacity. The sanctuary itself seats 1,000, but on High Holidays the foyer and assembly hall to the rear open to increase seating to 3,000. Even when open, the foyer remains exactly that—an anticipatory space to the main sanctuary. It is set off by sliding partitions, which in Mendelsohn's hands offer good sight lines when open. The vestibule feels like a secondary, but still ceremonially important space—rather than a social hall or other ill-suited space drafted in crises to seat latecomers and other peripheral worshipers.

Mendelsohn had begun designs for synagogues in Dallas, Baltimore, and Washington, D.C., that were never built. Like his first synagogue designs, they utilized a central court around which all the constituent parts of the complex faced. The sanctuary structure, especially in Dallas, is given the greatest prominence and the most forceful expression. The central-court plan and the relationship of sanctuary to ancillary buildings as worked out by Mendelsohn would remain extremely influential in American synagogue designs for decades.[13]

Opposite: The large sanctuary dome seems to grow out of the ground. It dominates the small daily chapel that projects from the tip of the building, like a ship's prow.

Right: The entrance to the complex from the side, behind the sanctuary (top). There are office and classroom spaces that surround a courtyard (bottom).

Bottom: View into sanctuary from social hall, through the then innovative use of sliding doors.

Top: Detail of the Ark wall in the main sanctuary, with Jewish symbols of Torah crown, blessing hands, and Decalogue superimposed on a menorah motif.

Opposite: The daily chapel is comfortable and well-lit, but the fixed individual seats are suggestive of a theater experience.

Below: Temple Beth Sholom, Miami Beach, Florida. The large arched window that separates the sanctuary from the vestibule is similar to the window type Percival Goodman used at Providence.

**Percival Goodman**

Mendelsohn's most active contemporary, and his greatest competitor, was the much younger New York architect Percival Goodman (1904–1989). In the 1940s Goodman, who would eventually become the most prolific synagogue designer in history, was experienced mostly in commercial design. He regularly confronted contemporary concerns of urban community and design. With his brother Paul he had published the social and architectural manifesto *Communitas* in 1947.[14] His interest in expressing community through architectural language, and his reaction to the Holocaust, led Goodman to synagogue design, helped by a series of fortuitous events.

In June 1947 the Union of American Hebrew Congregations (UAHC)—the association of American Reform congregations—sponsored a symposium in New York City to address the increasingly pressing needs for new synagogue construction in the postwar period. "An American Synagogue for Today and Tomorrow" provided a forum for architects, artists, rabbis, and Reform Judaism officials to share their ideas for what a modern synagogue should look like, how it should function, and what resources were available for its construction.[15] The symposium followed an article in *Commentary* magazine by architectural historian Rachel Wischnitzer, "The Problem of Synagogue Architecture." Goodman, along with art historian Franz Landsberger of Hebrew Union College, and architects Eric Mendelsohn and E.J. Kahn, were invited to respond. Their essays were published in June, almost simultaneous with the UAHC symposium. The confluence established Goodman, along with Mendelsohn, as an authority on synagogue architecture—though he never belonged to a synagogue, and had not yet designed one.[16]

Goodman addressed the New York symposium on the topic "The Holiness of Beauty," and made a great impression. His talk and subsequent interviews led directly to at least three commissions—for Baltimore Hebrew Congregation; Congregation B'nai Israel in Millburn, New Jersey; and Beth Israel in Lima, Ohio. Shortly after, he was hired by Rabbi William G. Braude to design a new synagogue for Temple Beth El of Providence, Rhode Island; they settled on Goodman after a lengthy search in which several accomplished synagogue architects, including Charles R. Greco, Eric Mendelsohn, and Fritz Nathan, were considered.[17] The congregation liked that Goodman was Jewish and American. He had been recommended to Braude by German émigré Stephen Kayser, curator of New York's Jewish Museum, for which Goodman had renovated the Warburg Mansion. This experience had allowed Goodman to identify more as Jew, and to confront his own ignorance about the basic tenets and history of his religion. Kayser considered Goodman a better fit for Providence than his fellow German Jew Eric Mendelsohn. Art historian Meyer Schapiro, a medievalist who was also a champion of New York modern art, also recommended Goodman to Rabbi Braude.[18]

At Congregation B'nai Israel in Millburn, New Jersey, Goodman pioneered the integration of modern art into synagogue design. Works by several artists in a wide variety of media were placed throughout the synagogue building, on its exterior and interior, and many of these were made integral components within the architecture itself. Sculpture, murals, and textiles added color and texture accents to Goodman's designs, which themselves used a mix of materials.[19]

On the exterior of the Millburn synagogue is an abstract lead-coated copper sculpture by Herbert Ferber, said to be the burning bush.[20] A large mural by Robert Motherwell with visible Jewish symbols dominates the small vestibule.

A brick wall in the prayer hall contains a memorial niche with two small cornerstones from synagogues destroyed by the Nazis in Mannheim. The inscription reads: "To the heroes and martyrs, the known and the unknown who died for the sanctification of the Divine Name." The memorial—commemorating recent and horrific events—nods to the past, but also to the cultural destruction that frees the architect to embrace an ahistoric design. Goodman said on many occasions that it was the Holocaust that made him a Jew. Here, in his early synagogue of Millburn he places a tangible link to an old synagogue tradition, but more importantly acknowledges the event that transformed his life, and the lives of all Jews.

Modern art was only one of Goodman's lasting innovations at Millburn. He translated the modernist building vocabulary, which had been primarily used for industrial and commercial design and then avant-garde residential buildings, into a language appropriate for religious buildings. With a projecting panel—the niche of the Ark—and windows patterned like a Mondrian painting, the facade at Millburn reveals its modernity.

## Temple Beth El
## Providence, Rhode Island

Percival Goodman
1954



Simultaneous with Millburn, Goodman designed the large synagogue complex in Providence for the Reform Temple Beth El, a project much closer in nature to the work of Mendelsohn. For the new synagogue Goodman clearly broke with the past—he created a nonmonumental religious center in marked contrast to the Roman temple form of the congregation's previous home. The new synagogue is relatively low and unassuming, articulated on the exterior by broad, gentle arches that define the vaulted sanctuary. The directness of the design reflects in no small degree the approach of Rabbi Braude, who championed the project, and immersed himself not only in the details of choosing an architect, but also in helping the young architect find his way.

The signature element of Beth El is the sanctuary vault, which is simultaneously great and grounded—without the excess drama of Mendelsohn's designs. It rises from the walls and returns to them, sheltering the congregation beneath. At most, it can be seen to rise from the Ark wall and *bimah*, spreading the Torah, and the words of the rabbi, to the congregation.

Most of the exterior walls are made of brick trimmed with limestone. The traditional language of religious architecture has been dispensed with. Today the synagogue, set on a corner site, can be mistaken for a high school or a sports complex.

According to historian George Goodwin: "As a modern building, Beth-El lacks the solemnity, and perhaps the authority, of traditional religious architecture. It is physically and emotionally accessible, however. The temple is orderly but not stuffy, friendly but not chatty. It conveys a quiet dignity, eloquent in its understatement."[21]

One enters into a large foyer with a multicolor pavement. The foyer is a transitional space between outdoors and in, the secular world and the religious, and even within the complex between the everyday and festive. Large windows allow a clear view to the landscaped outdoors. The foyer opens into the meeting hall on the left and the sanctuary on the right.

The main sanctuary seats nearly a thousand. The wooden vault rises 32 feet, but appears higher. The diamond pattern of the trusses in the copper-sheathed vault create the primary decoration of the space. Clerestory windows, designed like Roman thermal windows, fill the space with shifting north and south light. Six hundred seats can be added to

Opposite: View of the main sanctuary, looking toward the *bimah* and Ark.

the sanctuary by opening the walls of eight classrooms on the north and south sides. At the east end is the raised platform of the *bimah*, which nestles the Ark. Given the size of the sanctuary, the Ark is a modest affair. Unlike Mendelsohn, Goodman allowed his Ark dignity, but he did not elevate it to totemic status.

As in Millburn, Goodman integrated modern art into his design. The clerestory windows are sandblasted with inscriptions.[22] Ibram Lassaw designed the bronze, skein-like columns that flank the Ark. Called *Pillar of Fire* and *Pillar of Cloud,* the columns were subsequently selected by the Museum of Modern Art for the 1954 Venice Biennale. David Hare created a Calderesque menorah, which appears to float to the left of the ark, and he also made the eternal light—originally designed to burn olive oil, but subsequently transformed to run on electricity.[23]

Opposite: From every spot in the sanctuary, the curve of the vault leads the worshippers eye to the *bimah* and the Ark.

Below: The main entrance to the synagogue is unassuming. The vault of the sanctuary, with its large window, is clearly visible on the right.

**Temple Beth El** Providence, Rhode Island

This page: Percival Goodman created a progression of lobby spaces (top left, bottom left) to separate the profane world from the holy. A series of doors (bottom left and top right) suggest the biblical command "Open the gates of righteousness, for me, that I might enter them and praise the LORD (Psalms 118:19).

Opposite: In the chapel the dome lights the *bimah*, which is set more centrally among the seats in a traditional manner. Here, as opposed to the more formal sanctuary, a small group of worshippers can feel close together.

## Temple Beth Sholom

### Miami Beach, Florida

Percival Goodman

1956



While the Providence synagogue was nearing completion, Goodman demonstrated his versatility by designing Temple Beth Sholom in Miami, Florida, begun in 1953 and finished in 1956. The Reform synagogue was founded as Beth Sholom Center in 1942, gradually attracted new members, moved to different quarters, and finally built its current facility in the 1950s at the corner of Chase Avenue and Arthur Godfrey Road. The Temple has grown in stages. The sanctuary and banquet hall were completed first, the religious school and auditorium were added in 1961; and in 1984, the school was refurbished and an administrative wing was completed.

In many ways this synagogue was a departure for Goodman, and overall it created a new vision for American synagogue design. The design owes a lot to Mendelsohn. A large concrete shell spans a prayer hall auditorium. From the rear, the building appears as a perfect low hemispherical dome, echoing Mendelsohn's great dome at Park Synagogue. Instead of a drum, however, the lower part of Goodman's dome is pierced by a series of parabolic arches. Some of these are filled with screens of interlocked Stars of David. Multicolor glass is set into scores of triangular and hexagonal windowpanes, allowing the interior to glow with color at all times of day. The Ark is placed in the easternmost arch, atop an eight-step *bimah*. The doors of the beautiful Ark depict the Tablets of the Law. The spaces around the bold letters of the commandments are cut away so light penetrates the Ark to reach the Torah scrolls within.

The building is not just a meeting space set under a dome, however. It opens wide to the west in a broad embrace of two sections of slightly curved sanctuary seating—holding more than seven hundred. A large screen wall of two parts—the lower of movable wooden panels, and the upper of a huge arched space that curves out divided into a series of vertical strip windows—separates the sanctuary from a vestibule. Beyond is the social hall, which can also be joined to the other spaces for extra seating.

From the entrance vestibule, the hall resembles an outdoor bandshell. The arched upper part of the wall equals the highest part of the sanctuary vault, and it looms a story higher than the vestibule and social hall, again recalling Mendelsohn's sanctuary at B'nai Amoona. Overall Goodman's treatment of all the elements is more playful than Mendelsohn's, and thus it seems right for Miami's beach culture. It evokes the white domed mosques or churches of northern Africa or Greece, while at the same time anticipating the futuristic designs of the 1964 New York World's Fair.

Right: The sanctuary of this Reform synagogue looked futuristic when it was built. It recalls Mendelsohn's great dome at Park synagogue, but the colored windows make it dazzle.

EXIT

Opposite: Detail of the sanctuary showing seating illuminated by the patterned stained-glass windows.

Top left: Covered walkway leading to the sanctuary.
Top right: Exterior of the sanctuary seen from the north.
Bottom right: A view through the vestibule into the sanctuary. Note that Goodman uses folding accordionlike doors to divide his rooms.

## Beth Sholom Synagogue
## Elkins Park, Pennsylvania

Frank Lloyd Wright
1957



Mendelsohn and Goodman laid the foundation upon which the modern synagogue developed. Frank Lloyd Wright (1869–1959) helped give the synagogue symbolic and sculptural form. Congregation Beth Sholom, designed by Wright in Elkins Park, Pennsylvania, a suburb of Philadelphia, is now one of the best-known synagogues in the world. Wright had been hired in 1953 to design the synagogue for the congregation, but he died in April 1957 just a few months before its dedication. Before his death Wright was intensely involved in this project—and engaged in a wide-ranging correspondence with the congregation's rabbi, discussing matters of Torah and symbolism as they pertained to the building's design.

The cornerstone was laid in 1957. Wright wrote, "At last a great symbol! Rabbi Mortimer J. Cohen gave me the idea of a synagogue as a 'traveling Mt. Sinai,' a 'mountain of light.' We chose white glass. Let God put his colors on. He's the great artist. When the weather is sunny, the temple will glitter like gold. At night, under the moon, it will be silvery. On a gray day it will be gray. When the heavens are blue, there will be a soft blue over it."[24] Rabbi Cohen had referred Wright to a commentary that described the Tabernacle as a "traveling Mt. Sinai"—which accompanied the Israelites in the wilderness.

Beth Sholom's hexagonal plan is perceived more as a triangle because the steel supports for the soaring pyramid emerge from three strongly defined angles. Wright likened the plan to a pair of hands cupped around the congregation. "When you go into a place of worship, you ought to feel as if you were in the hands of God."[25]

Just as he sought new forms to express the essential qualities of Judaism, Wright sought out new materials to allow this expression. The building is a tripod of steel beams, faced with stamped aluminum, rising to an apex 100 feet above the floor. The tripod carries a double wall of translucent panels—white corrugated, wired glass outside and cream white, corrugated plastic inside. The two panels of glass and plastic filter the sun's glare. The origin for the structure and its symbolism can be found in Wright's unexecuted 1926 proposal for a Steel Cathedral. Thirty years later Wright returned to this concept to create a "luminous Mt. Sinai."[26]

The tripod rests securely on a vast concrete and reinforced steel bowl. This base gives real solidity to the entire structure, and also transmits the rootedness that is essential to the earthly aspect of Mt. Sinai,

Left: Interior of the sanctuary with the *bimah* set beneath a "mountain of light."

instead of the heavenly character of lightness and spiritual symbolism of illumination.

There are two levels to the synagogue, with the ground-level entrance set between them. From the vestibule, where the full expanse of the translucent pyramid can already be seen—drawing one upward—ramps ascend to the sanctuary. Steps descend from the vestibule to the chapel and lounges below, where pragmatic concerns, such as coatrooms and toilets, are met.

In the large sanctuary the eye is immediately drawn to the *bimah*—the raised platform that juts into the congregational space. The Ark is a centrally placed monolith suggestive of the Tablets of the Law (Decalogue). Light from within the Ark seeps through the glass border around its doors—a material representation of the illumination of the Torah.

Also set into the monolith, above the Ark proper, is a large frieze meant to dramatize the vision of the prophet Isaiah in which the prophet saw the Temple walls open and the likeness of God shine like a great light upon him. "The Seraphim, the Flaming angels, crowded about God's presence. . . . They veiled their faces from the Divine Presence [and] sang, "Holy, Holy, Holy, is the Lord of hosts; The Whole earth is full of His Glory" (Isaiah 6:3).[27] On the Ark, above the angels' wings, is the Hebrew word for Holy (*Kadosh*), three times, each word set over the other like an echo.

A huge, multicolored triangular glass chandelier hangs in the center of the space. It appears to be descending from the sky, which is visible around it, in changing hue, through the pyramid. The chandelier emits red, yellow, blue, and green light upon the congregation below. Rabbi Cohen bestowed a Kabalistic (mystical) meaning to these colors: blue represents wisdom; green, insight or understanding; yellow or gold for beauty; red, strength, courage, and justice; and white represents mercy and loving kindness. In the rabbi's words, "These variegated colors flow out of the great White light, the Eternal, the En-Sof, that is God."[28]

Wright had written, "The solution to every problem is contained within itself. Its plan, form, and character are determined by the nature of the site, the nature of the materials used, the nature of the system using them, the nature of the life concerned and the purpose of the building itself. And always a qualifying factor is the nature of the architect himself."[29] At Beth Sholom, the building grows out of the central idea of the synagogue as an expression of the need for communion between man and God. Thus, Wright chose the symbolism of Mt. Sinai,

where Moses confronted God, and God gave man the Torah. Added to this symbolism is an awareness of the description of the Tabernacle given in the Book of Exodus. In front of the Tabernacle stood the Laver, where the priests prepared themselves before entering. At Beth Sholom, Wright and Cohen recalled this tradition by placing a fountain before the doors. More explicit symbolism can be found on each of the three ridges of the synagogue, where seven protrusions are interpreted as menorahs—the Menorah also was present in the Tabernacle.

As in many of Wright's buildings, the synagogue is designed as a whole—from furnishings down to lamps and door handles. This unity generates energy that infuses the entire structure. Rather than creating a decorative system that is repetitive and predictable, the marvelous details perpetually surprise and delight. The Ark, the menorah, the pulpit, the chandelier, and the memorial tablets are a reflection of this principle.[30]

In this design Wright cast off all traditional forms of synagogue architecture and especially the complacency of the Classical tradition, the style of the congregation's previous home. In the words of architecture critic Bruno Zevi, Wright's architecture, exemplified in this building, represents "the victory of time over space that is the architectonic incarnation of Jewish thought, all the more significant because it has been realized by a non-Jew. . . . Like Schonberg's music, Wright's architecture is based in linguistic polarity, emancipated dissonance, contradiction; it is at once Expressionistic and rigorous."[31]

Opposite: After the small main entrance, similar to that of the nearly contemporary Guggenheim Museum, the effect of the soaring interior space is surprising, and awe-inspiring.

Above: An exterior fountain reflects the shape of the synagogue; its placement also recalls advice from the Talmud to place the synagogue near water.

Opposite: The interior of the synagogue epitomizes critic Bruno Zevi's evaluation that Wright's architecture is "expressionistic and rigorous."

Above: A huge triangular chandelier hangs in the center of the sanctuary space. Rabbi Cohen assigned mystical meanings to the colors.

## Congregation Kneses Tifereth Israel
## Port Chester, New York

Philip Johnson
1956



Soon after Wright was engaged to design Beth Sholom, another ambitious modernist took on the task of synagogue design. In 1953, Philip Johnson (b. 1906), the United States' foremost promoter of the International style, received the commission for a new synagogue for the Congregation Kneses Tifereth Israel, a Conservative congregation in Port Chester, New York, not far from Johnson's hometown of Greenwich, Connecticut.[32] The building was dedicated on June 3, 1956. Johnson's architectural views were quickly being accepted into the mainstream—due to both corporate America's embrace of modernism and Johnson's efforts to become a favored architect of corporations. But he was an unusual choice for this—or any—synagogue because of his fascist political beliefs in the 1930s.

In a previous design for a church in Greenwich, a commission that Johnson ultimately did not receive, a dome hung over a central altar surrounded by circular rows of seats. An elliptical foyer was nearly independent of the sanctuary, connected only by a short hall. The church design was a departure for Johnson, a first step away from the rigid International style designs he had favored. Learning that the congregation in Port Chester was about to design a new synagogue, Johnson came forward and offered his services without charge. This bold move was hard to reject, and Johnson received the commission. Johnson was thus able to transform his church concept into a synagogue.[33]

In the catalog for an exhibition on American synagogues that opened shortly after the completion of Kneses Tifereth Israel, Johnson spoke of a very practical approach to synagogue design:

> The problem of designing the contemporary synagogue is a nearly impossible one. It would not be so if only the sanctuary were the problem. Religious space has always in history been the most exacting and pleasurable to build. The Parthenon and Chartres Cathedral, perhaps the greatest architectural temples of the West, are religious buildings. A Jewish temple is as great a problem. The difficulty comes from the habits of the High Holy Days, when the attendance, shall we say, swells. Now a space is either great small or great large, but it can hardly act like an accordion and be great small and large. How to

Right: Seen at night with light shining through the hundreds of colored windows, the normally blocky exterior takes on the appearance of a glittering jewel box.

design a room that will be great both ways? Our solution at Port Chester was a great room, with a small screen divider, because it seemed to us that most of the congregation comes only on High Holy Days and we wanted the community to enjoy the temple. Once this hurdle is crossed, the design of a synagogue is the finest problem in architecture, a space where awe and reverence are the prime considerations, an inspiring challenge to the artist. The shoulds and shouldn'ts of design from this point in are the architects' business. The temple as a problem, unlike many Christian churches, is open to talent. The Southern Baptist Church, for example, must have a Colonial steeple. The Jewish temple merely has to be beautiful. As simple as that.[34]

Kneses Tifereth Israel is a beautiful building, like an eloquent jewel box.[35] Instead of a gem-studded exterior for its boxy form, the well-proportioned building is marked by 286 slit windows of colored glass that are laid in an irregular rhythm. The outside during daylight is intriguing but plain. The white, precast concrete of the walls glistens and emphasizes the sharp lines and angles of the form. At night, however, when services are held and interior lights are on, the building comes to life as a vibrant grid of color. Inside, the effect is reversed. By day, shafts of colored light stream inside, sometimes crisscrossing to create an interior luminosity—intense but serene. One imagines being caught inside a rainbow. The effect is less extreme than at Goodman's Beth Sholom in Miami, designed at almost the same time, because the windows here are smaller and less regularly spaced.

The entrance to this lightbox of a synagogue is through an elliptical vestibule, lit by a skylight, set in the middle of the building's long south side. This element is retained from Johnson's earlier church design as a transitional space between the profane and sacred, the everyday and holy day (holiday). The vestibule is like the decompression chamber of a submarine, where the air is changed. Johnson, however, places no meaning or symbolism on any aspect of his design. In a 1986 letter to the congregation, the architect wrote, "There is no symbolism here since, at that time, thirty years ago, there was not as much interest in symbolic architecture as there is these days. . . . In other words, the domed vestibule is merely a domed vestibule."[36] Johnson, of course, was being coy. He knew very well as Kneses Tifereth Israel was being built that he was racing Frank Lloyd Wright, who made no bones about announcing the symbolism of his "mountain of light" in Elkins Park.

Johnson's interior space is a clean, spare hall divided by black steel structural supports into seven bays. The bays are emphasized by the plaster canopies that appear to hang from the ceiling like suspended cloth. Skylights above these canopies project diffuse light throughout the interior. The soft curves of the ceiling place the building in the long tradition of religious basilicas with long naves divided into vaulted bays. Though there are no side aisles here, the repetition of the bays emphasizes the longitudinal thrust of the space. This is not obvious, because entry to the synagogue is from one of the long sides. Johnson's configuration goes back to antiquity—to Roman buildings like Trajan's Basilica Ulpia and other buildings used as law courts, markets, and other secular spaces. There is a tradition in synagogues, too, of sanctuaries being entered from the side, such as at the medieval synagogues in Worms and Prague, or in the Renaissance Scuola Canton synagogue in Venice.[37] The false vaulting of the bays can also be seen to suggest the temporary architecture of tents and thus the detailed description of the building of the Tabernacle given in the Book of Exodus.

Because there is little detailing other than the colored windows and the ceiling canopies, it is difficult to gauge the scale. In fact, the sanctuary is deceptively big, with a capacity to hold 1,000 worshipers. Partitions framed with aluminum and steel bracing allow the size to be adjusted.[38]

The *bimah* is a raised platform at the east end of the hall. A simple stage, with steps on the sides, it elevates the clergy and congregation leaders, but does not enthrone them. The oak Ark, lectern, reading table, and chairs were designed by Johnson to match the

Opposite: Entrance to the sanctuary is from a long side, through an elliptical vestibule. The trees surrounding the building were not Johnson's idea.

Opposite: View of the sanctuary looking from the *bimah*. The size of the seating area can be adjusted by moving the interior wall along a bay system articulated by steel supports visible in the side walls.

Left: Detail of the side walls showing a pattern of slit windows of colored glass.



austerity of the sanctuary. The Ark is a simple freestanding wooden chest with flat bronze letters mounted on its doors. The fact that the Ark is not part of a larger, architecturally designed wall installation, encourages the comparison of the synagogue to the ancient Tabernacle. Two older chairs on the *bimah* come from the congregation's previous synagogue, and two other chairs have been added.

The *bimah* features religious art designed by Egyptian-Jewish sculptor Ibram Lassaw (b. 1913).[39] It offers some relief from the relentless purity of Johnson's design, but it also in its own way asserts the Tabernacle association, especially through the rugged form of the menorah of hammered bronze, in which Avram Kampf saw "the divine evoked by the grotesque." Kampf continued:

> It stands, like a stage prop, waiting for the drama to begin. . . . It evokes an image of the first menorah fashioned by the biblical sculptor Bezalel, who used a crude mallet and still cruder cutting tools. Like his menorah, this one is expressed in a form that is stark and striking. It reflects the light of the desert, the burning sun, the texture of the sand and the scorching wind.[40]

The stand and candle holders of this menorah represent strength and timelessness—two qualities associated with the menorah because it continued to burn throughout adversity, and because, as an enduring symbol of Judaism, it has signified both sacrifice and hope to generations.

Lassaw began to make abstract sculpture in the 1930s, and over the next two decades he strove to create a formal balance between geometric and organic form. For Congregation Knesseth Tifereth Israel he designed an eternal light that appears like a metallic sunburst. It hangs off center, to the left of the Ark. A large screen of welded copper, bronze, and aluminum wire forms a backdrop to the *bimah*. The intricate wire pattern appears as a graffiti-like drawing against a white painted backing. This work, entitled *Creation*, measures 12 by 34 feet and projects one foot out from the wall plane. Lassow described the work as "a symphony structured in space rather than sound . . . an offering I praise and wonder of the living universe . . . inspired by the starry fields, the galaxies and galactic clusters of Which we are a part."[41] One can view Lassow's ethereal ordered disorder as an antidote to the inspired, but still stolid geometrism of Johnson's modernism. Similarly, one can view it as the chaos of creation out of which God created the order of man's thought and action, described by the laws and traditions of Judaism, and embodied in the purpose and form of this synagogue.

The early 1950s were a period a great experimentation for American synagogue architects. In the next decade the pace of work would be maintained, and even bigger projects would go forward. The basic language of contemporary synagogues was, however, substantially in place. Congregations would be asked to choose between modest functionalism or dramatic symbolism.

Above: Plaster canopies appear suspended over the congregation like cloth, connecting this sanctuary to the Tabernacle described in the Book of Exodus. The apparent soft curves of the canopies are a striking contrast to the hard lines and right angles throughout the rest of the sanctuary.

Opposite: The *bimah* and Ark repeat the simple geometry of the space. Ibram Lassow's sculpture on the Ark wall provides relief from the relentless purity of Johnson's design. Note the sunburst eternal light hanging off-center to the left and the rough menorah far right.

EXIT

# Chapter Six

## Baby Boom and Building Boom (1955–1970)

The path of the righteous is like radiant sunlight,
That shines more and more until the perfect day.

—Proverbs 4:18

Lawrence Hoffman, professor of liturgy at the Hebrew Union College-Jewish Institute of Religion in New York, has written: "By the 1950s the American synagogue began to resemble a local Chamber of Commerce organized by entrepreneurial merchants. . . . Congregants did not expect to share personal problems or even socialize with one another. The synagogue had become the congregational equivalent of a 'limited liability community,' one which occupied only a little corner of the members' larger lives."[1] In recent years the monumental, often impersonal synagogues of the immediate postwar decades have been accused of serving as an apology by congregations for their withdrawal from other manifestations of Jewish life and of turning people away from real devotion and spirituality.

Certainly, other factors in postwar American society were strongly tugging at Jewish sensibilities to homogenize and regulate religious behavior. Just as in the mid-nineteenth century a buzz word in American Jewry was *decorum*, in postwar America people talked about *acceptance*.

At the end of the 1950s tension was increasing within the American Jewish community about what was an acceptable mix of secular and Jewish life. As baby boomers came of age in the 1960s many turned away from organized Judaism. Some, however, worked to transform the synagogue. Eventually terms like *decorum* and *acceptance* were heard less while such new words as *community*, *spirituality*, *tradition*, and *transformation* took hold.

This chapter showcases the range of synagogue design possibilities pursued in the late 1950s through the early 1970s. Big was still good, but increasingly, big was not enough. Beginning in large part with innovations in Modern Orthodox synagogues, which were normally smaller than their Reform and Conservative counterparts, modern architects began to craft a new language of intimacy and community.

Opposite: North Shore Congregation Israel, Glencoe, Illinois. The south wall of the sanctuary shows how Minoru Yamasaki was able to use technical innovation to startling aesthetic effect and to link the sanctuary to the natural landscape.

Above: Chicago Loop Synagogue, Chicago, Illinois. Exterior view with sculpture by Henri Azaz.

שמע ישראל יי אלהינו יי אחד

## Chicago Loop Synagogue
**Chicago, Illinois**

Loebl, Schlossman & Bennett

1958

The Chicago Loop Synagogue, in the heart of Chicago's business district, was one of the more unusual synagogues built in the 1950s. The first synagogue of the small Orthodox congregation, founded in 1929 to serve the religious needs of downtown businessmen, was destroyed by fire. The building's replacement was designed by Loebl, Schlossman & Bennett for the lot next to the previous site, and was dedicated in 1958. The architects had only a narrow city lot and a limited budget with which to work. Although the congregation's religious outlook and service are traditional, the design of the space is decidedly modern.

Daily worship is held in a *beth-midrash* (study room) on the ground floor, which also houses offices, coatroom, and lavatories. A ramp ascends to the main Sabbath sanctuary on the second floor, obviating the need for an elevator, the use of which is prohibited on the Sabbath.

Entering the sanctuary one looks directly to the east wall: an enormous stained-glass window designed by Abraham Rattner (1895–1978) that fills the entire wall and allows maximum light into the sanctuary. The theme of the colorful design is, appropriately, "And God Said, Let There by Light and There was Light."

According to the artist, "I tried to make this design a reflection of the presence of God through the shimmering light of the stained glass for I wanted very much to succeed in creating an atmosphere of contemplation and meditation where man might experience that feeling of hope and a renewed faith in a higher elevation of being."[2] The spatial configuration of the sanctuary is unusual. The Ark is set in the corner, so that the congregants can face east as required by Orthodox practice, but most seats face north to a solid wall against which the *bimah* is set.[3] More seats, set further west, and a balcony over these seats, are angled to face northeast to view *bimah*, Ark, and stained-glass east wall.

According to architect Richard Marsh Bennett (1907–1996), the space conveys a sense of dignity and "eternity" despite the simple, inexpensive materials. Cutting standardized granite blocks into irregular shapes created "rusticated" interior walls to recall the West Wall of the Temple Mount in Jerusalem. Hand-wrought metal work adds an artisanal effect.[4]

The success of Rattner's window initiated a vogue for large, abstract stained-glass window installations in synagogues. Hundreds of stained-glass commissions were executed for American synagogues over the following two decades.[5]

Left: The second floor sanctuary of this Orthodox synagogue is dominated by the wall-size stained-glass window by Abraham Rattner, which symbolically and practically celebrates the creation of light.

## Temple B'rith Kodesh
### Rochester, New York
Pietro Belluschi
1962



Italian-born architect Pietro Belluschi (1899–1994) moved to the United States in 1922. He began to practice architecture in Portland, Oregon, in 1925, and continued to work there until 1951, when he became Dean of Architecture and Planning at MIT. Belluschi's commercial work is represented by the International-style Equitable building of Portland (1945–48). His religious buildings were quite different in approach. He designed many churches and five synagogues, which together comprise a remarkable body of work. Belluschi's religious structures are relatively modest in scale and adopt vernacular and traditional motifs to create comfortable, warm, and well-lit community spaces. Where his commercial buildings celebrate technology, Belluschi's religious buildings are decidedly natural and low-tech. When Belluschi left Oregon he was already one of the foremost church designers in the United States. While at MIT, and later in retirement, he continued to design, and it was in these late years that his synagogue work took form.[6]

In 1959 Rabbi Philip Bernstein and the congregation of Temple B'rith Kodesh in Rochester, New York, commissioned Belluschi "to design a large complex of religious and educational buildings on a spacious, flat, 15-acre landscaped site in an affluent residential neighborhood of Rochester, New York."[7] Belluschi designed a 65-foot-tall, twelve-sided domed sanctuary that rises above a cluster of simple one- and two-story buildings.

The sanctuary seats 1,250 and is entered through a broad loggia that leads to a quiet, landscaped courtyard. As in Eric Mendelsohn's plan for B'nai Amoona (chapter 5), the courtyard physically separates prayer and educational facilities, but visually connects them.

The synagogue is a steel-frame structure with low sidewalls of warm, rosy brick over which rises the dome. Its sides are glazed, screened by panels of stained redwood. The sanctuary is vaulted by a tall, framed structure of bent steel beams that meet in an oculus. Narrow, convex panels of sound-absorbing redwood screen the space between the structural ribs so that the sanctuary reads as a screened structure similar to the traditional Judaic tent. The high dome with center oculus is reminiscent of the Pantheon in Rome, where Belluschi was in residence when he designed the building. Like Albert Kahn before him (at Beth El, Detroit), he was immensely moved by the simple geometry and the dramatic play of light of the round Roman temple form. The

Right: The dome of the sanctuary.

twelve sides are a specifically Jewish reference to the Twelve Tribes of Israel. Throughout much of the design process Belluschi imagined that these panels would carry decorations making the numerical symbolism more specific.

While certain features of B'rith Kodesh thus refer specifically to Jewish sources, Belluschi used many similar motifs in his churches as well. He said:

> There is no architectural tradition to match the Jewish faith. Architects can contribute to a trend by creating spaces that serve their purpose with clarity and nobility. By emphasizing the special nature of simple materials such as wood and brick, they may achieve beauty without ostentation and with economy of means. The architecture of the synagogue should be an eloquent expression of the spirit of man.[8]

While the sanctity of the space is mostly expressed through the use of natural materials and the focusing of light, there is one prominent artistic statement in the complex—a massive bronze Ark by sculptor Luise Kaish (b. 1925). This large work is composed of a collection of figural panels representing key moments of man's confrontation with God as gleaned from scriptural passages. In its size and medium, and in its central location, this Ark is surely one of the major works of Judaica of the past half-century. Indeed, it is the culmination of an artistic journey of Kaish, who in the years previous had sculpted scores of smaller bronze figures representing biblical scenes. Rabbi Bernstein visited Kaish, a former congregant, at her studio in Rome on his return from Israel just before planning of the new synagogue began. When the time came to design the Ark, Bernstein recommended Kaish to Belluschi, who, after meeting the young sculptor, agreed and gave her free reign for her design.[9] She transformed an early idea of designing a giant bronze door in the tradition of Italian medieval doors that she loved. Even today, the presence of Kaish's figures on the Ark is an exciting shock. In an act of balance, Belluschi commissioned Richard Filipowski, a colleague from MIT, to design an abstract welded metal Ark in the chapel.

Above: The tall redwood sheathed sanctuary contrasts with the horizontal lines of the office wing.

Opposite: Massive bronze Ark by sculptor Luise Kaish.

אנכי יהוה
לא יהיה
לא תשא
זכור את
כבד את
לא תרצח
לא תנאף
לא תגנב
לא תענה
לא תחמד

Above: The daily chapel with an abstract Ark by Richard Filipowski.

Opposite: The sanctuary looking toward the Ark.

## Temple Oheb Shalom
### Baltimore, Maryland
Walter Gropius
1960



Established in 1853, Temple Oheb Shalom (Place of Peace) was originally located in South Baltimore.[10] When the Jewish population moved northwest, the congregation relocated to its second home, which became known as the Eutaw Place Temple. During the congregation's centennial year, 1953, it acquired a suburban site and completed the move to Park Heights Avenue in 1960.[11] Walter Gropius (1883–1969) in collaboration with Sheldon I. Leavitt designed the building. Like Mendelsohn, Gropius came from Germany, but he was neither Jewish nor a refugee. As chairman of the Department of Architecture at Harvard University after 1938, Gropius infused the American architectural mainstream with his passion for modernism. His influence led directly to the eclipse of the Beaux-Arts style in the United States after World War II. Gropius had no prior experience designing synagogues, and there was little in his past that suggested an affinity with sacred space. Thus, his plan for Oheb Shalom utilized others' recent synagogue center innovations, and his design, which has now been substantially altered, looked toward industrial architecture for inspiration.[12]

Gropius's Oheb Shalom conformed to designs that were popular at large, new suburban synagogues in the 1950s and 1960s. It linked sanctuary, social hall, meeting rooms, administrative offices, and a classroom wing in one connected facility. A central south-north spine ran from a projecting entrance porch, through a long lobby/vestibule, past a small courtyard, through an office wing, and then to the almost detached school area. A large parking lot was set beyond the school at the farthest distance possible from the sanctuary. The worship space was given primacy on the campus. It is the largest, tallest, and most articulated element, and almost the first space one encounters when entering.

In his address at the dedication of the new synagogue, Gropius described the role of architecture in lofty terms:

> Here begins the realm of architecture, which is to give form to what stands behind our practical daily activities: our ardent desire to search for the meaning and purpose of life. A temple should induce in us a

Right: Exterior view showing the original entrance with the sanctuary on the left and the social hall on the right. In Gropius's design, the two spaces could be connected across a vestibule.

TEMPLE OHEB SHALOM

> receptive contemplative state of mind; it should promote meditation; it should lift our thoughts onto a spiritual plane.[13]

Despite these words, and perhaps his intention, Temple Oheb Shalom was not particularly effective in promoting contemplation or in lifting thoughts to a spiritual plane. The sheer size of the sanctuary and the excessive height of the *bimah* imposed a hierarchy that precluded communal intimacy. The lean modernist lines and the hard materials employed also worked against spiritual uplift and religious awe.

Unlike many of their contemporaries who were designing synagogues at the time, Gropius and Leavitt appear to have deliberately avoided some the expressiveness apparent in the synagogues of Mendelsohn, Frank Lloyd Wright, Sydney Eisenshtat, Minoru Yamasaki, and others. Writing in *Architectural Record*, Leavitt used much of the same language that synagogue builders had used a century earlier, when the still evolving Reform movement emphasized *decorum* and *dignity* as a primary goal for new sanctuaries and the religious services that took place within them. "Thus the sanctuary is clothed in dignified forms which yield strong, solid shadows," he wrote. "Its roof, in spaced measures, vaults to a great height. The auditorium exhibits a more temporal appearance but retains a suitable dignity of form to make it compatible with the sanctuary; this relationship is intimate when the spaces are combined."[14] Surprisingly, he mentioned functionality—normally a defining element of the modern architecture that Gropius championed—only in relation to the classrooms and the administrative block, which "express their practical plans and academic uses by crisp straight lines and extensive use of glass." Practicality was important here, as the school was designed to serve nine hundred students. Its hardy construction consisted of slab-reinforced concrete floors and roof, and glass and precast concrete with exposed surface aggregate for the curtain walls.

Gyorgy Kepes designed the glass mosaic murals on each side of the entry. Leavitt explained their role: "They provide an immediate introduction to the spiritual content of the temple; their transparent colors, grading from dark to light, symbolize the passage from daily activities to the realm of religion."[15] Today, however, these mosaics are hardly seen, because the former entryway has become a rarely used, vestigial space.

The most prominent element in Gropius's design, repeated within and without the synagogue, is the Decalogue—the tall, arched stone tablet upon which the Ten Commandments are usually depicted,

Opposite and above: The shape of the large Decalogue on the outside of the original Ark wall of the sanctuary makes the connection between the Commandments and the Ark within, but also with the shape of the vaulted bays of the sanctuary itself (opposite).

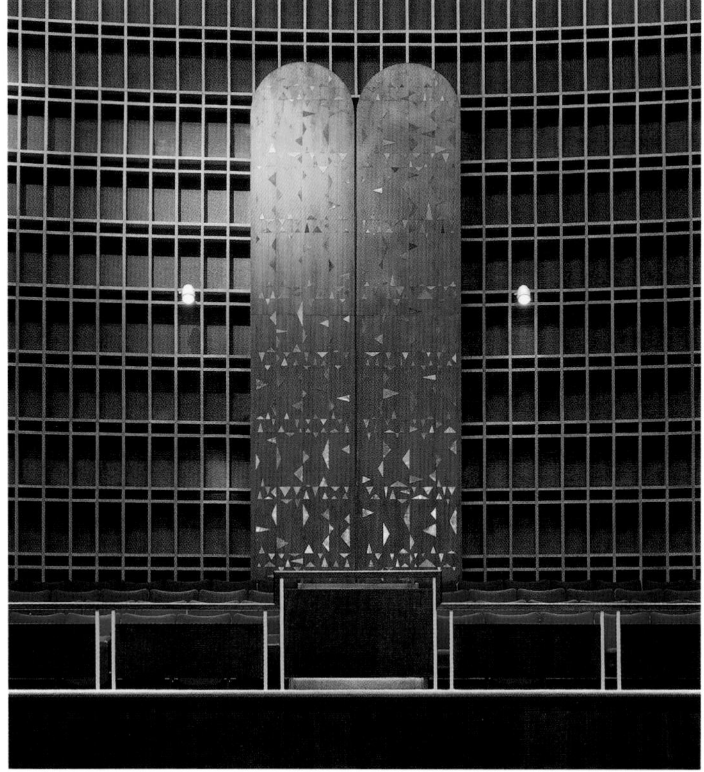

representing the laws given by God to the Jewish people through Moses on Mount Sinai. On the synagogue's exterior there is an explicit representation of the Decalogue on the east wall. Inside, the main bulk of the sanctuary itself is expressed in a series of barrel-vaulted sections aligned to create a sequence of seven bays—four of which are expressed as tall arched segments—looking like single wings of the typical Decalogue tablet. This arrangement has also been likened to industrial turbines, certainly recalling the AEG Turbine Factory by Peter Behrens in Berlin, a work that influenced Gropius and modern architecture.

Above: The original tall Ark and high *bimah* are still in place, but as part of a raised seating area in the rear of the sanctuary, where the orientation has been reversed in a recent renovation.

The original lobby of the synagogue, which separates the sanctuary to the left and the social hall/auditorium to the right, was low, so that upon walking into the 40-foot-high sanctuary one experienced the relief of the great rise in space. The sanctuary roof is a series of 15-foot-diameter vaults without any interior supports. One of the notable features of the sanctuary, now changed, was the upward grade of the floor, which created a gradual sweep toward the *bimah* and Ark that, in turn, generated a feeling of ascent. The configuration ensured a clear view of the *bimah* from all 1,100 sanctuary seats, and from the adjacent auditorium that was used for add-on High Holiday seating, which doubled the seating capacity.[16] Nonetheless, the upward sloping floor was never popular with the congregation, and was reversed in the recent renovations, so the seats now face the opposite direction.

Lighting in the sanctuary was intentionally subdued to create, in the words of Leavitt, "the mood of the sanctuary as one of reverence. Everywhere the source of light is obscured or indirect and always it is subdued. Sunlight does not enter the building directly."[17] There were few windows in the building, in order to separate worshipers from the outside world, but skylights did brighten the Ark. These skylights are still in place, but the Ark has been moved to the opposite end, so now they provide general, ambient lighting. A stained-glass clerestory spanned the rear wall, hardly seen by the congregation. Now it tops the Ark wall and has become a major decorative element.

The original Ark wall of the sanctuary consists of a high, wide, and slightly concave wooden gridded screen that is colored gold, with a beige fabric stretched behind it to separate the choir seating. This screen was broken up only by the 20-foot-tall Ark, in the shape of tablets, designed by Kepes and Robert Preusser. The doors of the original Ark (still in situ) are walnut veneer with an appliqué of triangular bits of metal.[18] Several large sculpted menorahs were set on the *bimah* against the background grid of the Ark wall. One of these—a copper and cloisonné enamel menorah, also by Kepes and Preusser—is now on the new *bimah*.[19]

Top left: Levin/Brown remodeled the sanctuary, placing a new *bimah* in what was rear of the hall. Now the congregation looks up and sees the original windows which were previously ignored. New false arches have been inserted spanning the width of the hall between each of the original barrel-vaulted segments.

Bottom left: Remodeled sanctuary showing new *bimah* and Ark, beneath stained-glass windows in what was previously the sanctuary rear wall.

Below: One of a series of engraved plaques newly installed in the sanctuary which mark the Jewish holidays. This one celebrates Rosh Hoshanah, the Jewish New Year.

## Temple Sinai
## El Paso, Texas
Sidney Eisenshtat
1962



One of the most sculptural synagogues of the 1960s is Temple Sinai in El Paso, Texas, designed by Sidney Eisenshtat (b. 1914) for a Reform congregation. Jewish presence in El Paso dates to 1879, but a formal congregation was not founded until the arrival of Rabbi Oscar J. Cohen from Mobile, Alabama, in 1898. The first synagogue was dedicated in 1899. Indicative of the ecumenical nature of American small towns, clergy from at least three different Christian denominations participated in the synagogue dedication ceremony. A few years later the congregation affiliated with the Union of American Hebrew congregations. By 1916 the congregation had grown considerably and moved to a new building.

Forty years later, the congregation was ready to move again. This time, a more spacious center was planned to accommodate all the now-required functions of a modern Reform congregation. The congregation turned to California modernist Sidney Eisenshtat, who had designed Temple Emanuel in Los Angeles in 1954. Eisenshtat was commissioned to create a space that was both functional and expressive, a task he achieved by integrating simple dramatic forms into a harsh but beautiful desert landscape.

The main part of this complex was completed in 1962. One enters from a parking area through an open walkway into a paved multi-level courtyard. To the left is the chapel, a round bastion supporting the walkway roof. On this is inscribed (Psalms 121:1), "And I will lift up mine eyes unto the mountains." Looking up, one sees the stark surrounding hills.

Diagonally across the courtyard is the entrance to the sanctuary. A wall to the right of the entrance is inscribed (Genesis 28:17), "This is no other than the house of God." This wall is the rear of an office and classroom wing that looks out through a screen of open patterned tiles, onto a second courtyard on the other side. The tiles filter light onto a long corridor. The sanctuary soars, a parabolic concrete shell that from afar resembles a tent, an appropriate form recalling the Tabernacle in the desert. The concrete construction harks back to B'nai Amoona in St. Louis and Beth Sholom in Miami (chapter 5). But here, the dramatic setting in an arid landscape gives greater expressive force to the design, making it believable as the historic-mythic natural form of Mt. Sinai.

Right: View of the entrance courtyard looking toward the sanctuary.

THIS IS NONE OTHER THAN THE HOUSE OF

Top: View from the parking area into the entrance court.
Bottom left: Second courtyard with classroom and office wing on the left.
Bottom right: Corridor of classroom and office wing with tiled wall that allows light to filter in from second courtyard.
Opposite: The sanctuary looking towards the Ark.

Opposite: Southeast wall in sanctuary lit by recessed panels of colored glass.

Top: Sanctuary interior, view from the *bimah*.
Bottom: The interior of the chapel.

## North Shore Congregation Israel
## Glencoe, Illinois

Minoru Yamasaki
1964



Frank Lloyd Wright's design for Beth Sholom broke the mold of modern synagogue design. Wright was an avowed modernist, but not a rationalist. He was comfortable injecting expressionistic and symbolic motifs into his synagogue design. Wright in his idiosyncratic way was a deist—he felt the power of the divine in the natural world. He also, more than his predecessors, even Mendelsohn, set out to create an architecture that was clearly sculptural in its formal massing—so much so that despite his disclaimers about functionality, the sculptural and symbolic aspects of his "mountain of light" became the dominant and memorable characteristics of the building.

In the 1960s, it was Minoru Yamasaki (1912–1985) who most dramatically continued the evolution of synagogue, carrying on from Mendelsohn and Wright. Others, like the more rationalist Percival Goodman, also adapted their styles in response to Wright. And architects as diverse as Max Abramovitz, Peter Blake and Julian Neski, and Sidney Eisenshtat carried on this expressionist/sculptural trend.

Yamasaki, best remembered for designing the World Trade Center in New York, designed two synagogues for Reform congregations. In 1959, he was commissioned by North Shore Temple Israel to design a new synagogue for its lakeside site in Glencoe, Illinois. North Shore Congregation Israel was founded in 1920 by families whose goal was "an interest in furthering their thought and creating a background of Jewish thought for their children."[20] These families were mainly members of the Classical Reform Sinai Congregation, which held services on Sundays, in accordance with most of the Reform congregations in the Chicago area at that time. By the late 1950s, the need for larger facilities became obvious, and a congregant acquired the magnificent property overlooking Lake Michigan in Glencoe where the present synagogue was built.[21]

The synagogue is one of the most striking designs of the postwar years—daring in its technical and structural innovations, triumphant in its spatial configuration, and breathtakingly beautiful in its landscape setting. The large sanctuary of this synagogue and Yamasaki's second synagogue commission for Congregation Beth-El in Bloomfield Township, Michigan, are modern versions of the so-called cathedral synagogue—social, if not stylistic, heirs to large axially and hierarchically arranged nineteenth-century American synagogues such as Emanu-El in New York (1868) and Sinai Temple in Chicago (1875–76), and the later Temple Emanu-El in New York of the 1930s (chapter 4).

Right: View of the *bimah* and Ark.

Left: The expressive exterior of the sanctuary is juxtaposed with a simpler entrance wing, a glass-walled walkway that connects to other parts of the complex.

Opposite: The open ark.

Yamasaki called North Shore Congregation Israel "an interlacing of daylight and solids."[22] North Shore was his first religious structure, and he appears to have approached the task as he would a new airport terminal. The technical challenge appealed to him more than the need to create a sacred place. This approach had its limitations in creating a spiritually fulfilling space, but it also liberated Yamasaki from many formal constraints of traditional synagogue architecture.

It is interesting that by the early 1960s, the axial arrangement of a sanctuary, shared vestibule, and social hall, promoted by Percival Goodman in many of his designs, was already considered the norm, and Yamasaki rejected this cost-saving trend. He explained:

The usual solution for the expansion seating of a synagogue on the High Holy Days is to combine the sanctuary with an auditorium and open the space between the two. This solution is an undesirable one from many standpoints. It makes for an esthetic hodge-podge to combine a spiritual space with a functional one. It poses severe acoustical problems when the two are used separately and simultaneously and it creates circulation hardships. The expansion of this sanctuary is provided through two means. The main sanctuary area is made large by having platforms on either side of the main seating that tie in with the bema platform at the front. The additional space provided by these platforms on the sides gives a sense of spaciousness to the sanctuary. The lobby is larger than needed for circulation and, as the memorial hall, provides expansion space and makes it suitable for other functions.[23]

The sanctuary is enclosed by eight pairs of reinforced concrete fan vault shells weighing more than 90 tons per pair. The skylights diffuse the light through amber glass. At night, a system of dimmer-controlled incandescent and fluorescent lighting, installed between the inner and outer panes of the skylights, performs this role. Leaded-glass panels in the end and sidewalls provide accents. A choir loft is reached by a stair in the rear of the sanctuary. A surrounding platform at windowsill height can be used for expanded seating on the High Holidays.

Like many of Yamasaki's other designs, spaciousness overwhelms the individual worshiper. In the 1980s the congregation built a new, smaller sanctuary designed by Thomas Beeby, in a more intimate style (see chapter 7).

יהוה
ואהבת

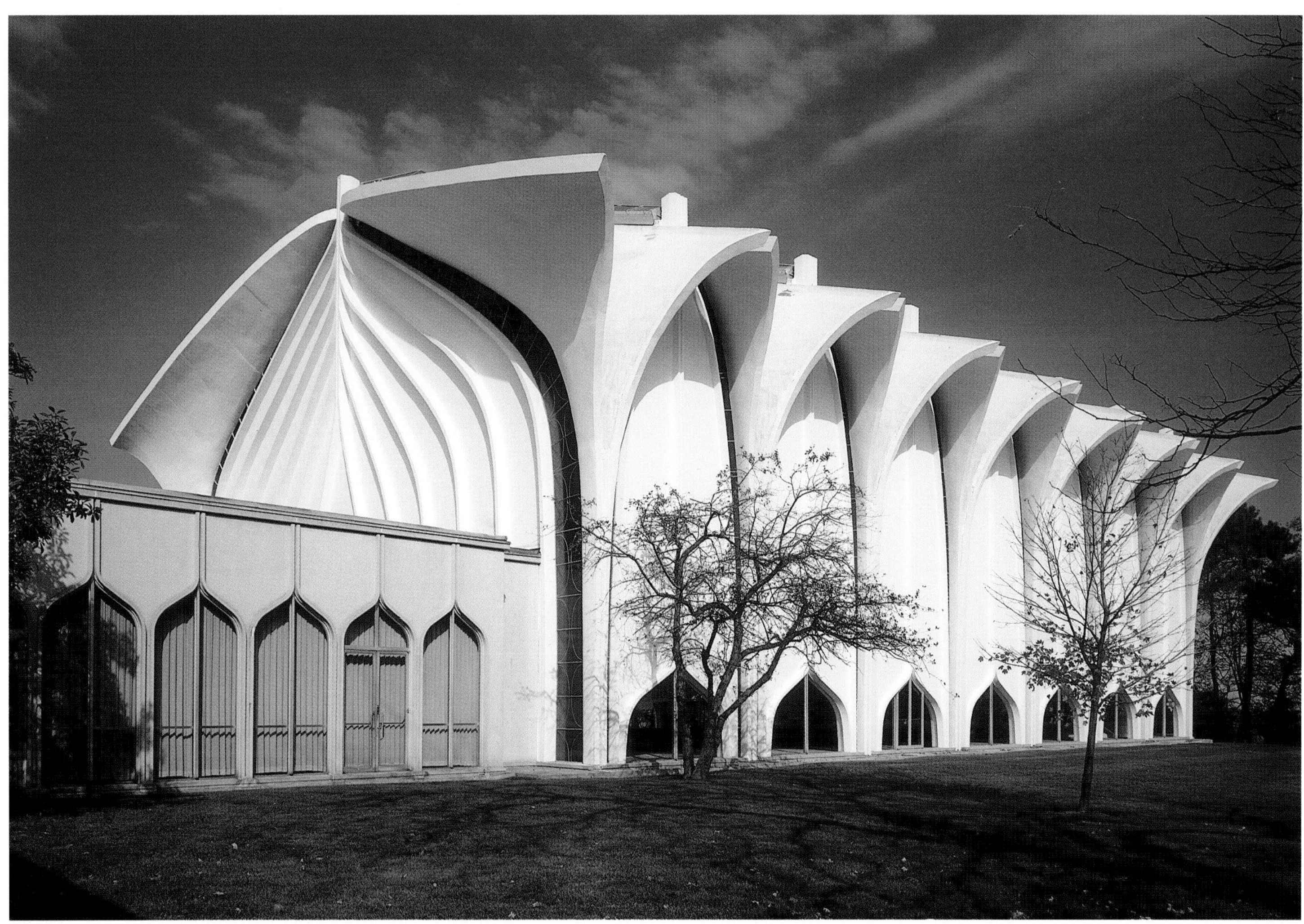

Opposite: The appearance of the sanctuary shifts throughout the day, as light filters in from different windows, creating new patterns of light and shade.

Above: Exterior. The entrance vestibule is on the left.

## Temple B'nai Jehudah
## Kansas City, Missouri

Kivett & Myers
1967



The search for sculptural expression and technical innovation witnessed in the work of Eisenshtat and Yamasaki culminates in a series of synagogues completed in the late 1960s. Of these, B'nai Jehudah in Kansas City, Missouri is perhaps the most striking for its exterior profile, its massing, and its combination of natural and industrial forms that merge primeval nature with futuristic design.

The congregation, founded in 1870, is the oldest Jewish congregation in the Kansas City metropolitan area. It has always been a Reform congregation, and was among the thirty-four founders of the Union of American Hebrew Congregations (UAHC) in 1873. From 1957 to 1967, when the size of the congregation increased dramatically, the congregation built its fourth home, located at 69th Street and Holmes Road. Construction by the local firm of Clarence Kivett (1905–1996) and Ralph Myers began with a new religious school, social hall, and chapel. The sanctuary was designed and built from 1965 to 1967. Today, with membership at about 1,700 families, the congregation is relocating to a substantial campus in suburban Overland Park.

Again, the motif of the tent provides the starting point for this project. In this case the canopy rises in a spiral of translucent blue plastic panels set in a steel frame tied to an 83-foot concrete center pole. The sanctuary is distinguished from the rest of the complex by its size, shape, position, and materials. From outside, it seems settled, like a spaceship that has landed near the highway.

The interior is a vast, open space that recalls Wright's light-filled sanctuary of Beth Sholom, but it encapsulates that light in an architectural frame that seems to spring upward in a swirl of movement. But unlike Wright's "mountain of light," which is stable, even static, the inside of B'nai Jehudah is on the move. And yet, despite the drama, the interior is quite simple. The center pole supports the Ark. Curtains draped around the low rear sections of the space can be opened to reveal expanded seating. The seating is a central plan, but the *bimah* is pushed to the edge, set around the support pole. On the *bimah* are a large bronze menorah, an eternal light, and the Ark itself, all designed by Norman Brunelli, a local artist.

Right: Exterior view.

לא תרצח אנכי יהוה
לא תנאף לא יהיה
לא תגנב לא תשא
לא תענה זכור את
לא תחמד כבד את

Opposite: View of the sanctuary interior with Ark inset into center supporting column.
Above: Detail of the Ark designed by Norman Brunelli.

Top right: Hallway with stained-glass windows taken from an earlier building.
Bottom right: The entrance lobby with large Hebrew letters of the word *Chai*, meaning "life."

## Temple Beth Zion

**Buffalo, New York**

Harrison & Abramovitz

1967



Wallace Harrison (1895–1981) and Max Abramovitz (b. 1908) were highly successful advocates of an elegant modernism in the postwar years, and they soon became favorite architects of the Rockefellers and many other institutional patrons. Abramovitz, being Jewish, was more drawn to Jewish communal and synagogue projects. The firm's first buildings in this genre were two Hillel Centers on university campuses in Evanston and Champaign, Illinois, built in 1951 and 1952.[24] These centers featured round-ended chapels surrounded by an arcade of reverse tapering columns, and a central open court around which meeting rooms and offices were placed. The chapels were small, though the Champaign building allowed for an expansion of the space for holiday seating.

These designs owe much to the overall configuration of parts laid out by Mendelsohn at B'nai Amoona, but the style of the Harrison & Abramowitz buildings is a cool, clear modernism without the emotionalism that Mendelsohn imparted to his sanctuary designs. The buildings were scaled to human use. Unfortunately, they were not built to withstand local weather conditions, and the center in Evanston was replaced by a new sturdier structure in the late 1990s.

Temple Beth Zion in Buffalo, New York, was founded as an Orthodox congregation in 1850, but had allied itself with the Reform movement by 1863. The following year, the young congregation moved to a former Methodist Episcopal Church on Niagara Street. Edward A. Kent designed a new imposing domed synagogue on Delaware Avenue dedicated in September 1890 that was used until it was gutted by fire in 1961. A new synagogue center, built just a short distance up Delaware Avenue, was designed by Max Abramovitz and dedicated in 1967. Over the decades, the 1891 synagogue had been enlarged with classrooms and other facilities so that at the time of its destruction it formed a substantial complex. The rebuilding attempted to re-create this mix of uses through an integrated design.

Abramovitz created an expressive masterpiece, one of the few fully uplifting emotional responses to architectural modernism in the United States. It differs greatly from his Hillel Centers of the 1950s. The building, which in the words of a contemporary critic appears "at once ascetic and Baroque," stands in stark contrast, in its underlying humanism, to many contemporary Brutalist-style buildings that use

Opposite: View of the sanctuary from the rear. The curve of the balcony accentuates the outward tilt of the walls.

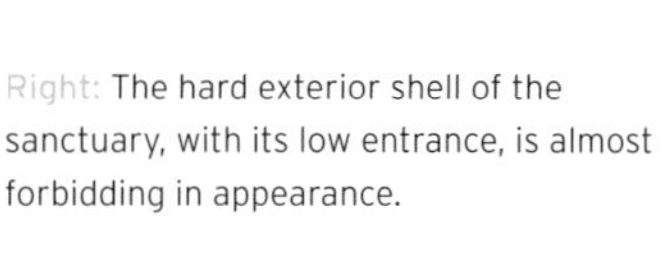

Right: The hard exterior shell of the sanctuary, with its low entrance, is almost forbidding in appearance.

Opposite: Ben Shahn designed the stained-glass windows, as well as the mosaic decoration on the massive Decologue panels flanking the Ark.

similar materials.[25] The brush-hammered concrete of the synagogue is closer to the rough surfaces of buildings by noted Brutalist Paul Rudolph or Le Corbusier's Chapel Notre-Dame-du-Haut at Ronchamp than to the smooth concrete forms of Louis Kahn.

From the outside, the building appears bowl-shaped. The impenetrable Alabama limestone walls flare outward as they rise, and are shaped with ten scallops per side. The main entrance is from Delaware Avenue, though today, it is more common to enter the sanctuary from behind the Ark, through a lobby that joins the space to the larger synagogue center. Above both of these entrances are large stained-glass windows, each an inverted wedge that breaks the sanctuary's solid shell.

The Delaware Avenue entrance is a low doorway under one of the large windows and a projecting flat canopy supported by two tapering columns. The austere entrance and severe solid exterior walls may intimidate some worshipers. The stained glass—the closest thing to a facade on the building—was designed by Ben Shahn and depicts, through colored calligraphy, Psalms 150, which was sung at the dedication of the first Temple on Delaware Avenue in 1890.[26]

The colorful composition is remarkable in many ways, but unfortunately, when not lit from within, it is hard to read from the outside—and appears more as a black void than as an instructive and celebratory artwork. Inside, the window is divided by the landing of the stairway to the balcony, thus it cannot be seen in its entirety.

Moving from the cramped vestibule through low doors, one enters the sanctuary where the ceiling rises to a height of over 60 feet. It seems to hover, suspended as a taut canopy stretched across the bowl

א
ל
ל
ז
כ
ל
ל
ל
ל
ל

Opposite: The view behind the Ark, revealed to those entering the sanctuary from the lobby of the synagogue center.

Left: Detail of the decorative calligraphy for the Ten Commandments and the Ark curtain.

Right: Glass and brass menorah on the *bimah* is also designed by Ben Shahn.

Above: Sanctuary interior and balcony.
Opposite: Chapel.

of the worship space. The edges of the ceiling are not flush with the walls. Light from hidden skylights filters through the open spaces, falling along the sloping walls to reveal a range of earthy colors in the rough concrete. A big balcony sweeps from the back of the sanctuary all the way to the Ark, where it meets two 30-foot concrete pylons flanking the Ark, holding it in a pincer-like embrace. These massive towers splay out across the *bimah* to stand as sentinels guarding the Ark. They are inlaid with mosaic tile that forms Hebrew letters designed by Ben Shahn, representing the Ten Commandments, the essential words of Jewish law.

The towers frame the synagogue's second huge stained-glass window, set behind the Ark. Like the front facade window, this is also designed by Ben Shahn as a large inverted wedge. With his famous calligraphic technique, it symbolizes the story of creation. Looking closely, one can discern an enormous upturned hand that molds primordial chaos, and the passage from Job (38:4–7) that gives architectural expression to the creation of the universe and to the building captions the scene:

Where were you when I laid the earth's foundations?
Speak if you have understanding.
Do you know who fixed its dimensions
Or who measured it with a line?
Onto what were its bases sunk?
Who set it cornerstone
When the morning stars stand together
And all the divine beings shouted for joy?

As if illuminated by the colored light from the Creation window, a large glass and brass menorah shines on the *bimah*, and a simple multifaced eternal light is suspended from above.

As already mentioned, many people enter the sanctuary from behind the Ark, utilizing parking facilities and the synagogue-center complex (which includes a museum, social hall, classrooms, offices, and other public spaces), and encounter Abramowitz's design somewhat in reverse. However, this eventuality was anticipated from the start, and the

wall behind the Ark is much more dramatic than from the formal entrance. One passes through a narrow passage, squeezed between massive concrete walls. Looking up, the walls, window, and Ark towers veer away. Light filters through the stained glass, from an ocular skylight above the Ark. The effect of this passage from profane to sacred space is magical.

* * *

### Modern Intimacy

Gargantuan dramatic statements were not the only design solutions for synagogues in the 1950s and 1960s. An alternative, especially embraced by Modern Orthodox congregations, was to create small, often understated worship spaces. This tradition is expressed in the (unbuilt) work of Louis Kahn; Davis, Brody & Associates; and Werner Seligmann, and continues to have a strong impact on the conception and design of synagogues today.

**Temple Beth Zion** Buffalo, New York

## Congregation Sons of Israel
## Lakewood, New Jersey
Davis, Brody & Wisniewski
1963



The Orthodox synagogue for Congregation Sons of Israel in Lakewood, New Jersey, was designed for use by a resident population and Orthodox visitors to the many resort hotels along this main street. The program called for a sanctuary to seat 350 people (men and women separate), expandable to 700 for holidays and special occasions; a social hall, with a stage, to seat 300 for dining; separate kitchens for meat and dairy food preparation; lounges and meeting rooms; and offices.

The resulting synagogue by Davis, Brody & Wisniewski (later to become Davis, Brody & Associates) takes advantage of a difficult site and incorporates a traditional plan and decorative elements with new features to facilitate function and to emphasize the nature of the worship service. From the outside, the building appears as a compact mass on a central (octagonal) plan. It is built on two levels, with the sanctuary in the upper portion. The roof profile is reminiscent of Polish synagogues with adjacent "annex" buildings. The architects explained their approach to the building's design:

> Although there is no historical tradition of synagogue design, there are some strong traditions of worship and ritual. Traditionally, the synagogue is different from other places of worship in that it is basically a gathering place for laymen; priests are not required. The most important aspect of the service is the reading and studying of the Torah. We have, therefore, striven to express architecturally this unit of ritual and congregation by designing spaces, which have a central orientation, developing from the circle, the square, the octagon, rather than the rectangle. Our aim has been to emphasize the centrality and gathering of the congregation under one roof for worship in contrast to the usual axially directed space that sets up an audience to stage relationship.[27]

Rabbi Pesach Z. Levovitz led the Orthodox congregation at the time of the synagogue's construction, when he spoke of the transformation of a "passive audience into an active congregation." The synagogue service "is conducted by and for the congregation. While the rabbi and cantor officiate, the service is sanctified by the congregation's participation . . . regardless of his location, every worshipper experiences a sense of closeness to the *bimah*, which is the spiritual hub of the sanctuary."[28]

Right: A view along the central axis, through the centrally placed *bimah* to the Ark.

קול חתן וקול כלה
WALL OF KESER SHEM TOV
IN HONOR OF
AND MARION WERBLER
AND FAMILY
EXIT

To accomplish the rabbi's aim, the architects blended two synagogue forms that are among the most traditional and meaningful in the United States but had not previously been joined. The interior of the synagogue adapts the traditional Sephardic plan, the synagogue arrangement used in the earliest American synagogues, where two ranks of benches set against the north and south walls run the length of the building, and face each other across an open well that serves as a liturgical arena. At the east end of the building is the Ark, on a raised platform. In the standard Sephardic tradition, the *bimah* would be set opposite the Ark against the west wall, but here at Congregation Sons of Israel, the architects borrowed from the Ashkenazic (Eastern European) tradition and moved the *bimah* to the approximate center of the open space, closer to the Ark. The result is that all worshipers are close to the *bimah*, though some, especially those seated in the northwest and southwest corners, are far from the Ark.

The link to Eastern Europe is also seen in the shape of the building and the contour of its roof. Its octagonal plan and hipped dome roof recall the exterior profile of many now-destroyed Eastern European wooden synagogues. This was the view of the architects, who certainly consulted the influential book *Wooden Synagogues* by Maria and Kazimierz Piechotka, which had been published in English in 1959.

Levovitz saw additional meanings in the building's shape and plan. "The circular character of the sanctuary is symbolic of the eternity of our faith and the never-ending truths of Judaism. In the Jewish mystic tradition, the circle is a sign of infinity and eternity; for just as the circle has no beginning and end, so it is with God and our Torah."[29] He related that the center of the sanctuary, which appears sunken due to the stacked seating on either side, reflects Psalms 130, "Out of the depths have I called unto Thee Oh Lord." For the rabbi, the exterior of the synagogue "towers high into the sky, giving the appearance, at a distance, of two hands clasped in eternal supplication."

The central plan of Congregation Sons of Israel, and the traditional Sephardic placement of the Ark, *bimah*, and the seating arrangement make it difficult to expand the main prayer room to accommodate larger congregations, especially for the High Holidays. This is less of a problem for an Orthodox congregation than for a Reform one, since in

Above: The building profile recalls the form of many Polish wooden synagogues. A Hebrew day school is built next door.

Opposite: A memorial to victims of the Holocaust.

FOR THE DEAD AND THE LIVING WE MUST BEAR WITNESS
REMEMBER MY AFFLICTION AND MY ANGUISH
REMEMBER O LORD AND KEEP MY SOUL HUMBLE BEFORE THEE
REMEMBER, LET US NOT FORGET
WARSAW GHETTO MAJDANEK
BUCHENWALD TREBLINKA
DACHAU AUSCHWITZ-OSWIECIM
SOBIBOR BERGEN-BELZEN
"NEVER TO BE FORGOTTEN"
THIS MONUMENT REPRESENTS A SYMBOL OF MAN'S INHUMANITY TO MAN. IT STANDS FOR OUR SIX MILLION MOTHERS, FATHERS, SISTERS, BROTHERS AND PRECIOUS CHILDREN, VICTIMS OF NAZI TYRANNY, BRUTAL PERSECUTION AND MERCILESS WANTON MURDER 1939 — 45. WE DEDICATE OURSELVES TO THEIR MEMORY WITH A SENSE OF REVERENCE AND DEEP SORROW. MAY IT SERVE AS A SILENT WITNESS TO HISTORY NEVER TO BE REPEATED AGAIN.
FOR THESE I WEEP
MINE EYES DRIPPETH WATER
THE SECRET OF REDEMPTION
RESIDES IN REMEMBRANCE

an Orthodox synagogue it is expected that most members of the congregation regularly attend services year-round. In Lakewood, however, fluctuations in the congregation size result more from seasonal population changes, because Lakewood is a popular summer resort.

At Sons of Israel, small meeting rooms and a lobby are adjacent to the sanctuary. To enlarge the sanctuary for the High Holidays, wood-slat doors are rolled open on three sides of the sanctuary. The separation of men and women, however, dictates that the north and south extensions are solely for women, and only the west extension (the lobby) can serve men. The women sit in their own section behind the men's benches, separated by a low screen of Hebrew calligraphy with verses from *A Woman of Valor* (the last chapter of the Book of Proverbs). Unlike in many Orthodox synagogues of old, the women's accommodations are comfortable and in close proximity to the Ark and *bimah*, so that women can fully follow the service. The calligraphy of the screens is the work of prominent Judaica artist Ludwig Wolpert (1900–1981), who also created the cover of the Ark.

All of the art in the synagogue is simple but elegant. Because Orthodox Judaism strictly interprets the Second Commandment (forbidding all figurative and representational images), abstract designs and calligraphy fit comfortably not only within the architecture, but also within Orthodox values, laws, and beliefs. At Sons of Israel, the clerestory windows designed by Samuel G. Wiener, Jr., are especially noteworthy. Filled with colored glass panels they signify daily, weekly, and yearly Jewish rituals.

The sanctuary lighting is indirect. High-powered quartz lamps are aimed upward from the projecting cove under the clerestory, where they supplement the ring of colored natural light that infuses the dome. Overall, the lighting is quite simple, without the dramatic effects of so many contemporary modern synagogues.

Congregation Sons of Israel differs in another important aspect from many contemporary modern synagogues, especially the more sprawling suburban complexes of Conservative and Reform congregations. For a variety of reasons that include both the restrictions of the hillside site and the respect for tradition, Sons of Israel sits on a fairly small lot, and is built in two full and distinct levels, utilizing the site to better accommodate the plan. There is a long tradition, from the ghettos of Italy to the tenements of the New York's Lower East Side, of placing sanctuaries on upper stories of buildings. In some cases this was done for economy and security, but more often in recognition of a spiritual hierarchy that elevates the most spiritually important and uplifting space. This follows a Talmudic recommendation that a synagogue should be built on the highest place in the city.[30]

Thus, social facilities, which are subservient to religious obligations, are located on the lower level. "We felt this was desirable," explained the architects, "in that the dominant expression of the structure is that of a synagogue rather than a community center and more in keeping with the Orthodox conception."[31]

Opposite: Detail of Ark, with calligraphy by Ludwig Wolpert.

Above: This is the view of the Torah reader looking toward the Ark. The congregation has temporarily subverted the architects' plan by placing tables and chairs in the central space.

IN LOVING MEMORY OF
SIMON LENCH
שמעון בער בן יהושע
ג׳ כסלו תשנ״ו
OUR BELOVED HUSBAND, FATHER, ZADIE
WHOSE ENDLESS KINDNESS, LOVE & DEVOTION TO OTHERS
WILL NEVER BE FORGOTTEN
HE WILL FOREVER BE IN OUR HEARTS
PRESENTED BY
HIS CHILDREN
TOBI AND BEN KIRSCH

**Temple Brith Sholom**
**Cortland, New York**
Werner Seligmann
1969



German-born architect Werner Seligmann (1930–1999) created several synagogue designs in the 1960s that were tailored to the unique characteristics of the congregations they were meant to serve. Seligmann survived the Holocaust as a child (his mother and sister perished) and emigrated to the United States in 1949. He studied architecture at Cornell University, where he established a lifelong link to Central New York.

In Binghamton, New York, he built the Orthodox Beth David synagogue, a thoroughly modern structure that combined traditional arrangements, such as placing the 400-seat sanctuary on a second floor, and the inclusion of a small courtyard, with the use of inexpensive materials such as exposed block and concrete for expressive purpose.[32] The plan is remarkable in that the functional spaces serve as a foundation for the much smaller upper-level prayer hall. The result is like, in miniature, the artificial Mount in Jerusalem upon which the Temple perched.

Nearby, in the town of Cortland, where he lived, Seligmann received another commission for the even smaller Temple Brith Sholom, a nominally Conservative synagogue dedicated in 1969. Like Beth David, the project is a modest urban building on a small lot. The building is very private, however, and mostly looks in upon itself, in the manner of many small-town European synagogues, especially those from Seligmann's native Germany. The entrance to the low brick complex is off a parking lot set back from the street. Though the synagogue takes a defensive posture, the publicly presented corner offers a tantalizing mix of shapes and lines. Like the Binghamton synagogue, there is a small courtyard that creates a transitional mood.

The Cortland congregation, which consists of between thirty and forty families, is nonhierarchic and for most of its existence has not had a permanent rabbi or cantor. The building reflects this attitude—inside, all the spaces are united, though sliding panels can subdivide the space to isolate the small sanctuary. This space has a special purity. At first it appears simply boxlike, but shifts of floor level, lighting, and symmetry subtly charge the space with quiet energy. The low ceiling of the central all-purpose hall, through which one must pass, creates a pressure that is released in the sanctuary, where the floor slopes away and the ceiling rises.

The theatrics of Yamasaki or Abramovitz are nowhere to be seen. Instead, an upward sloping ceiling with a skylight and the nearly square,

Right: View of the sanctuary. The square Ark wall is framed with light.

אנכי יי
לא יהיה
לא תשא
זכור את
כבד את
לא תרצח
לא תנאף
לא תגנב
לא תענה
לא תחמד

white Ark wall that seems to float on a frame of light, are enough. The sanctuary has only six rows of pews, but it can be extended into the social area, from which one looks out through a glass wall to a sheltered garden.

This project was one that Werner Seligmann remained attached to throughout his life. His wife's family had been among the founders of the original Cortland community, and he lived in Cortland for more than thirty years. At Brith Sholom, Seligmann created a little known but emblematic statement of the balance between religion and community, modernism and tradition. Significantly, it is this same symbiosis that would dominate synagogue design at the end of the century, when many of the grand architectural statements of the postwar generation would seem obsolete.

Above: Entrance is through a small enclosed court (center). The sanctuary is on the left.

Opposite: Skylights illuminate the Ark.

אנכי ײ
לא יהיה
לא תשא
זכור את
כבד את

## Gumenick Chapel at Temple Israel of Greater Miami
## Miami, Florida
### Kenneth Triester
### 1969



A contemporary and equally distinctive but entirely different approach to synagogue design can be seen in Miami, where artist-architect Kenneth Triester was commissioned to create a chapel for Temple Israel, a large synagogue with a 1930s building in an eclectic Gothic-Deco style.[33] The design of the chapel, begun in 1962, coincided with the creation of an urban plaza by landscape architect Edward Stone, Jr. Triester designed the chapel and all the furnishings within it, so the entire space is a unified work of art, very expressive and personal, and highly unusual for a Jewish religious space.

Dedicated in 1969, its appearance very much reflects the artistic and social trends of the 1960s. According to Triester:

> An artist's ultimate goal is not only to create something beautiful, but also to lift subtly the spirits of those who experience his art. . . . The Chapel was created to increase the awareness of each congregant's relationship with God and his or her Jewish heritage. This chapel would celebrate the miracle of Jewish survival and the creativity of the Jewish people. The Chapel would follow the synagogue's traditional functions as both a religious and social institution. It would be a house of prayer (*beit tefilah*), a place for communal gathering (*beit knesset*), and a house of study (*beit midrash*).[34]

Despite these almost universal claims, the chapel functions mostly for special events such as weddings, bar and bat mitzvahs, and memorial services.

The chapel is conceived as a free-flowing sculpture, "a mystery without end."[35] Its exterior consists of a wall, pierced by large irregular windows filled with colored glass. The facade appears like a craggy cliff in the Judean desert where ascetic Jews took refuge, or where holy scrolls were hidden away for safekeeping. The sharp white light of Miami on the white stucco facade dazzles and twinkles in the sun, but hints at cool recesses locked within.

The influence of Triester's expressive forms can be seen elsewhere in Miami, notably Temple Beth Shmuel at 17th Street near Lenox in Miami Beach, home of the Cuban Hebrew Congregation. That building, designed by Oskar Sklar in 1984, has a dramatic facade—it too resembles a cliff dotted with cave openings, what one might expect in the desert near Qumran and the Dead Sea rather than in vibrant Miami Beach.

Left: Interior of the Gumenick chapel.

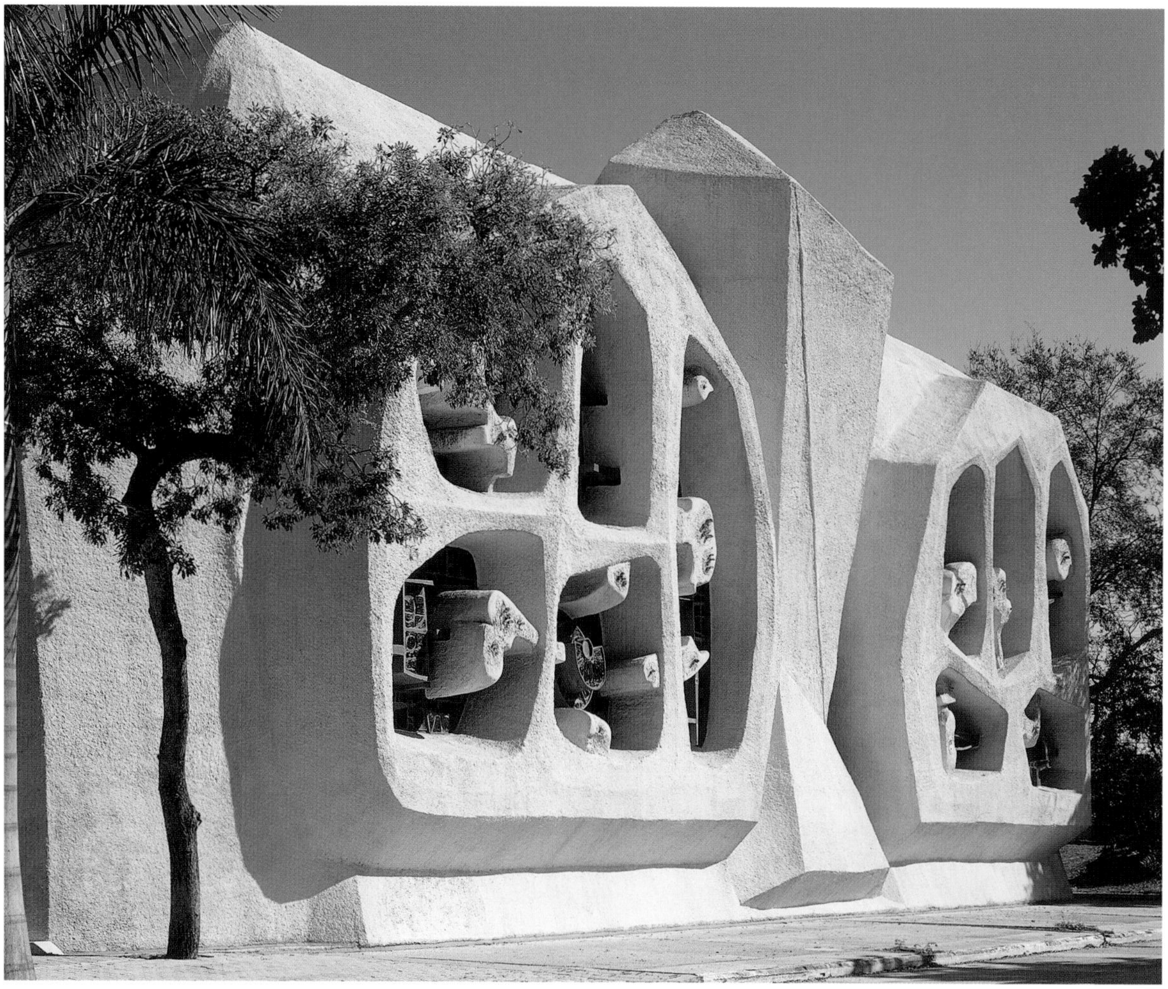

Above: Exterior of the Gumenick chapel.
Left: Exterior view of Temple Israel with Gumenick chapel joined on right.

Opposite: Interior of the Gumenick chapel. The brilliantly colored stained-glass windows, made by Benoit Gilsoul, are an integral part of the design.

Opposite: The interior of the chapel reflects Kenneth Triester's desire: "the creation of a total environment."

Above: Detail of one of the west stained-glass windows, set in black epoxy. According to their designer, the windows are meant to "cry in distress and . . . sing for joy."

דין
גדולה

# Chapter Seven

## Reflections and Recollections (1970–1990)

Open the gates of righteousness, for me,
that I might enter them and praise the LORD.

—Psalms 118:19

Following the boom years, a certain stability and even complacency could be found throughout the American Jewish community. Like much of the United States in the final years of the Vietnam War, institutional Judaism suffered an identity crisis. Having firmly inserted itself into the American mainstream, the Jewish community was no longer certain of where it was meant to go. Traditional Jewish religious, as well as political, values shifted as the exodus to the suburbs continued. Israel's 1967 victory in the Six Day War made it the focus of ethnic pride for American Jews. Ironically, this show of Jewish military might triggered a reexamination of the Holocaust, which had been ignored through the 1950s and 1960s. Both of these Jewish trends, as well as larger American social developments—especially the women's movement and the counterculture's increased interest in Eastern religions, meditation, and mysticism—affected every aspect of Jewish life, including synagogue design.

After 1973, big synagogue building projects declined, in part because of a national economic downturn, but also because demand had shrunk. Beginning in the 1970s, and continuing through the 1980s, resources shifted to constructing large regional community centers and to Jewish museums and Holocaust memorials. Simultaneously, some communities strove to re-create the lost intimacy of Old World and inner city synagogues. The congregations erected smaller chapels adjacent to their big sanctuaries. The new designs often harked back to recognizable historic styles, and many included symbolic elements referring to the lost synagogue culture of the Europe.

Many new congregations were formed. The traditional American tripartite segmentation of Judaism (Orthodox, Conservative, and Reform) was modified with the introduction of new liturgical variations, including the increased involvement of women in the service, an issue that divided many congregations. New congregations, often small and struggling, re-created (albeit unintentionally) the process of congregation building of the earlier immigrant populations. Their synagogues began as adaptations of existing buildings. In a few instances congregations began to restore older synagogue structures, committing to their use for another generation.[1]

Consideration of traditional synagogue forms—which first appeared in works of Davis, Brody & Wisniewski and other firms in the 1960s—continued as an undercurrent through the decade. Synagogues were not built to copy older designs, but certain traditional elements, including some for liturgical reasons and others for symbolic and aesthetic purpose, were selectively employed.

Not surprisingly, Conservative synagogues took the lead in this movement, and they had the strongest need to create a new architectural identity. Caught between tradition and reform in religious practice and in community organization, the movement never developed an architectural style of its own. Even the names of Conservative synagogues now failed to identify their mission, as more and more congregations came to refer to their synagogues as Temples—something previously limited to the Reform movement.

Opposite: Jewish Center of the Hamptons (formerly Gates of Grove Synagogue), East Hampton, New York.

## Temple Beth El of Great Neck
## Great Neck, New York

Armand Bartos & Associates
1970



The Temple Beth El synagogue complex in Great Neck, New York, occupies a hillside above a well-traveled road. It consists of an original prayer hall from about 1930, built in a collegiate Tudor style, that now serves as a chapel. A bland but functional social and educational building, erected in the 1950s, was burned in a suspicious fire in 1990s and is now being replaced by the architectural firm of Beyer Blinder Belle. The present sanctuary was dedicated in 1970.[2]

The congregation chose Armand Bartos & Associates as the architect for the new sanctuary. Bartos (b. 1910) had received extensive attention, especially in Jewish circles, for his design (with Frederic Kiesler) of the Shrine of the Book at the Israel Museum in Jerusalem in 1965.[3] The surge of pride in Israel within the American Jewish community that followed 1967's Six Day War was surely to Bartos's advantage in obtaining the commission. The new sanctuary is typical in many ways of the architecture of the late 1960s and early 1970s. These were years when many American institutions, such as universities and government agencies, adopted "fortress architecture"—blocky and severe on the outside, but light and open within.

The Beth El sanctuary is entered from the street through a low vestibule that quickly opens into a high and airy reception area lit by skylights. A substantial stairway climbs from this space, giving access to balcony seating. Stairs also descend to an expansive basement area that holds all the administrative offices. The sanctuary seats nearly 400 on the main floor, 130 in a riser section along one side that bridges the upper and lower galleries, and another 370 on the balcony. A movable partition opens onto a space that can hold an additional 370 seats. (This space is also used for receptions, such as the oneg shabbat.) On the High Holidays the social hall at the santuary's left can also be opened to bring the maximum capacity to 1,900—all within 100 feet of the *bimah* and with unobstructed views of the Ark.

Between the suspended ceiling and the roof structure is a canted skylight directing daylight onto the wide, stagelike *bimah*. A second skylight illuminates the rear wall of the balcony and directs light into the reception area. The close relationship between ceiling and seating patterns, and the use of uniform colors and material throughout, create a unified space that is elegant, but calm and unpretentious. The continuous

Right: Simple lines and colors unite the large sanctuary space.

זכרנו לחיים מלך חפץ בחיים וכתבנו בספר החיים

wooden balcony rail helps to visually tie together the entire interior and provides an accent to the monochromatic walls. The two skylights serve as illuminated "bookends" around the front and back of the sanctuary.

In addition to using a noted architect for its new building, the congregation also commissioned work from several leading Jewish artists, including a small Holocaust memorial relief by Nathan Rapoport just inside the doorway and a large wall sculpture by Louise Nevelson. Nevelson designed *The White Flame of the Six Million*, a relief that serves as the Ark wall and runs the entire width of the *bimah*. The long, white, flat cabinet seems repetitious but on close inspection one sees the many cutout wooden shapes are differentiated, curved and flamelike in memory of individual Holocaust victims. This is one of Nevelson's first works in a religious context and despite the size and location, it is more decorative and passive than many of her later religious commissions, such as her Becker Chapel for St. Peter's Church in New York (1977). The covers of the Torah scrolls were designed by noted textile artist Ina Golub.[4]

Left: Main entrance from street.

Above: The Ark, designed by Louise Nevelson, opens to reveal a collection of Torahs decorated with mantels designed by Ina Golub.

Above: Interior, view to Ark wall by Louise Nevelson, entitled *The White Flame of the Six Million*.

ליהוה

## Perlman Sanctuary at North Shore Congregation Israel
## Glencoe, Illinois

Hammond, Beeby & Babka
1979

By the late 1970s it was already apparent to many congregation administrators and religious leaders that the large synagogue sanctuaries erected in the 1950s and 1960s were inappropriate for many of the year-round needs of congregation, and were exceedingly expensive to maintain. During the energy crisis, the air conditioning and heating costs of these vast spaces became a problem. Many synagogue administrators complained that the upkeep of new materials, especially extensive areas of concrete and glass, was a growing problem. Water penetration was frequent in many new buildings only a few years after their completion.

Size became a burden. Many of the sanctuaries were designed to seat the maximum number of people expected to attend religious services on just a few days a year—Rosh Hoshanah and Yom Kippur. Often the numbers who would come to the synagogue on a regular basis for Friday night and Saturday morning services was a small fraction of holiday attendance. Even a few hundred people attending for a Friday night service in a vast hall could feel dwarfed and intimidated by the architectural setting.

From the start, some synagogues, such as B'rith Kodesh in Rochester and Beth Zion in Buffalo, had included smaller chapels in their architectural plans. Weddings, bar mitzvahs, memorial services, junior congregations, and many other religious services with smaller attendance demanded smaller, more intimate spaces. Increasingly, synagogues that had not made such a provision began to desire one.

North Shore Congregation Israel in Glencoe, Illinois, had built the dramatic synagogue designed by Minoru Yamasaki in the early 1960s (chapter 6). By the late 1970s, the congregation was ready for a more intimate worship space, and also a new social hall and kitchen area. Just as the congregation willingly embraced new forms and technologies for their first sanctuary, they chose to build in the newest American architectural style, Postmodernism, for their new prayer hall. Thomas Beeby (b. 1941) of the firm of Hammond, Beeby & Babka was chosen as architect.[5]

The new structures are integrated with the old, but set far off axis from the original sanctuary. In this way the new design neither competes with nor defers to the older sanctuary, which Beeby "did not regard . . . as a masterpiece," but which the congregation wished to respect.[6] The new building combines simple geometry—imbedding the circular plan of the prayer hall into a large rectangular space that includes the social hall

Left: Interior. The flexible seating is one of the important aspects of the space.

Opposite: View to the Ark. The use of rich draperies seems theatrical, but it has historical precedent.

Above: Entrance wall. Simple geometric shapes dominate the design.

addition. Within the cylinder of the sanctuary is imbedded a further cube. The spaces between cubic core and outer cylinder serve as ambulatories and support balconies. The use of traditional materials (brick and stone), classical ornament, and a lushly colored interior create a stark contrast with the earlier building. According to Rabbi Herbert Bronstein, who became rabbi of the congregation in 1972 and oversaw the expansion, "people wanted not only religious substance, they want a sense of sanctity."[7] Beeby looked to distant history to recapture that "sanctity." In addition to a certain spare geometry that is part of the Chicago architectural tradition, Beeby also responded to the lush interior spaces of the Sephardic synagogues of Venice, which are rich in classical detail, imported woods, gilding that shimmers in candlelight, and dark red draperies that give both elegance and mystery to the setting. In Beeby's solution, movable seating, however, allows different formats for prayer and meetings.

The result is full of laid-on classical arches and columns, but there remains, however, the feeling that plagues much Postmodern architecture—namely, that these elements are affixed to a box that, no matter how well concealed, exists very much on its own. Yamasaki looked for sanctity in formal grandeur, and though perhaps overblown, all the elements of his building were integrated. Beeby, on the other hand, looked for sanctity in a more appropriate human scale and the beauty of ornament. But rather than develop the ornament organically from the simple geometric form, he preferred its appropriation and application. This contrasts with the simplicity of Beeby's social hall, which offers a beautiful view of Lake Michigan. If the sanctuary owes more to Chicago's tradition of classical architects such as Daniel Burnham and synagogue architect Alfred Alschuler, then the social hall shows the influence of Chicago's buildings by Mies van der Rohe. This architectural pastiche is telling. In the end, the new sanctuary serves as a comfortable, but ultimately insincere, space.

## Jewish Center of the Hamptons (Gates of the Grove)

**East Hampton, New York**

Norman Jaffe

1989



No synagogue of the 1980s demonstrates more clearly the directions in which modern American Judaism has ventured—directions that, more than coincidentally, keep referring to past traditions while new forms of organization and new styles of worship are developed—than the Jewish Center of the Hamptons, also known as Gates of the Grove Synagogue, designed by Norman Jaffe and built in 1989. Nominally a Reform Congregation and affiliated with the Union of American Hebrew Congregations, the congregation is in many ways post-denominational, drawing its membership equally from Conservative and Reform communities and its practice from an even wider spectrum of Jewish sources.[8]

Architecturally, the building breaks with most recent precedents. It may be able to do this because of the hybrid nature of its congregation, which combines a community of residents with summer visitors (similar to the Orthodox Congregation Sons of Israel in Lakewood, New Jersey). The building draws on local vernacular and traditional Jewish sources in it use of wood, including its shingled exterior. It harks back to ancient models in its interior arrangement—where the hall is wider than it is long, a plan type sometimes referred to as the broad house synagogue. The synagogue seems, at first glance, sparse in decoration, suggesting a firm Modernist approach. Upon closer examination, however, one can find layers of symbols below the surface. One can enjoy this building without effort, but one must work to understand it—a reminder to those congregants expecting easy spiritual sustenance. Architectural historian Carol Krinsky writes, "It would be hard for anyone to spot the trees and Menorah without having been told that they were present, but the symbols are there for those who want them. Their abstract form allows one to ignore them in favor of the smooth texture and beautiful blond tone of the Alaskan yellow cedar that has been carefully crafted by master woodworkers."[9]

Perhaps the clearer symbolism is not in the overt signs of institutional Judaism, but in the omnipresent and overwhelming sense of nature that pervades the building and its grounds. Set in a grove of beautiful trees, visible from the main seating, and imbued with a wonderful sense of light, the synagogue defines Judaism as a spiritual balance as much as a historical force. The texture and color of the shingles relate this building to a rural tradition in the Old Country and in the United States. The use of wood immediately ties the building to the tradition of

Right: The sanctuary is broader than it is deep. The *bimah* projects into the seating, creating a more unified worship space.

חכמה

 wooden synagogues, but only in a general way; Jaffe was thinking of the Eastern European *shtetl*, but not imitating it. He tried to capture some of the mystical nature of light through the use of skylights. "Which is more important," he asked, "the light that falls on the *shtetl* or on Chartres or Westminster Abbey?"[10]

This building also recalls the architecture of Jewish summer resorts, such as those in Sullivan County, New York, and the Jewish agricultural communities of New Jersey and of course the Hamptons. Everything about Gates of the Grove is anti-urban, and in the American context, that is a deliberate sociological statement—a rejection of much of the previous century's Jewish identity. The congregants of this synagogue, many of them professionals from Manhattan, have indeed come a long way from the Polish *shtetl*, but also a long way from the austere formalism of Temple Emanu-El.

The building also rejects most of the developments of postwar American suburban architecture. There is no concrete or other hard materials, and nature is ever-present. The emotional charge of the place is due not to technological achievement, but to carefully crafted details and intimate space. Part of the beauty of the synagogue is an almost infinite variety. Though relatively few motifs are employed, their appearance changes from every position from which they are viewed.

The angling in the woodwork, what the architect Jaffe referred to as the "arches" is one distinctive feature. He compared these to an "an old Jew bent in prayer" and also to the shapes of Hebrew letters. Small but easily recognizable stars appear on the exterior, relieving the repetition of the shingles. From within, the view out of the sanctuary over the *bimah* through windows to greenery beyond presents a shifting panorama—not the familiar static Ark wall of older synagogues. This link to nature is not entirely new—Werner Seligmann tried to open his synagogue in Cortland (chapter 6) to nature—but before Gates of Grove it had not been handled so well.

Other parts of the building are open to interpretation. The sanctuary floor is made of irregularly cut pieces of limestone, roughened at the edges, meant, perhaps, to recall the stone of Jerusalem. Thus, the synagogue rises from a Jerusalem foundation.

The sanctuary plan forms a square set into a rectangle, with seating only in the broad rectangle. The *bimah* partially projects into this area, with seating on three sides. Here, too, the older synagogue forms come subtly into play. This space does not re-create a European synagogue, but it firmly breaks with the performer-audience arrangement dominant in American Reform and Conservative synagogues.

Inscribed into the sidewalls above seating niches are the names of the *sefirot* (virtues of Adonai, the Eternal One) described in the Kabala. We see here a move away from Jewish rationalism, which had been the mainstream of Reform thought for over a century.[11] References to a mystic tradition, and all sorts of greater spiritual values, are included in

Above: The synagogue relates both to its natural setting and to adjacent older architecture.

Above: Even at night there is a sense of transparency to the structure, as if it was a grove of trees.

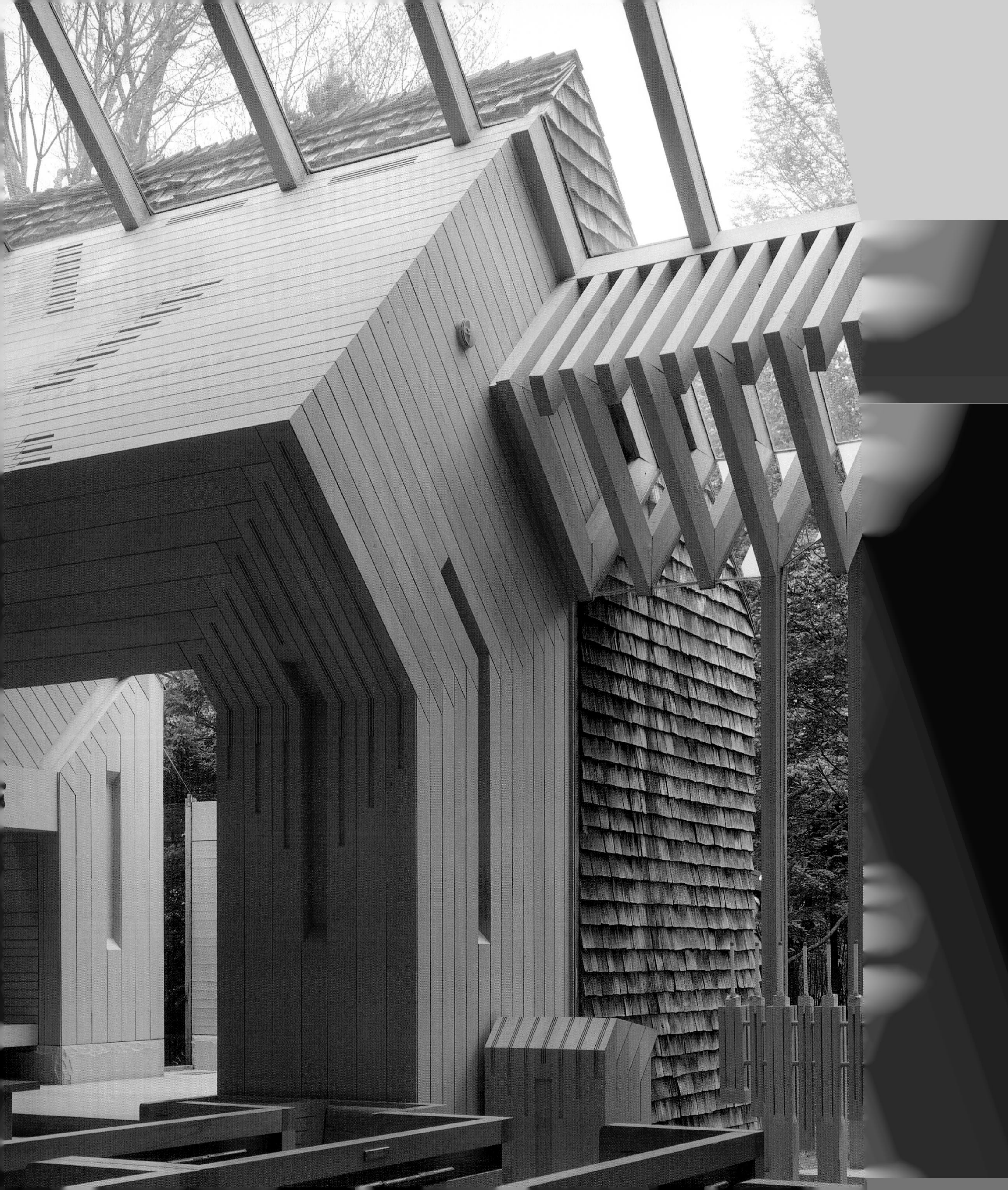

the synagogue design. In the 1980s, Jews were leaving the fold—not just leaving traditional Judaism through apathy and intermarriage, but actually seeking greater spiritual fulfillment. Zen Buddhism and other Eastern religions had great appeal for the post-1960s Jewish generation. New trends in architecture, as we can see at Gates of the Grove, and in synagogue programming and prayer, try to address this longing to find new spiritual satisfaction in a traditional Jewish setting.

The American synagogue sanctuary of all periods has mostly been entered through a small vestibule, a transitional area separating the everyday from the sacred. The use of a forecourt or narthex for this purpose goes back to synagogues and churches in antiquity. Norman Jaffe varied this tradition by designing a long entry corridor, which he called a "conditioning space to empty the mind of matters of the street."[12]

Rabbi David Gelfand, referring to the congregants, noticed in 2000 that "there is something that happens either as people come through the midtown tunnel or into the Pine Barrens, when they take the mindset of their suit off and the intensity of the city. . . . The beauty of the Hamptons fits with a sense of spirituality that is very prevalent in our culture at this time."[13] Jaffe was able to anticipate and inspire this sense of spirituality in this design, prefiguring the dominant trend in synagogue architecture in the decade to come.

Opposite: The use of wood links local and "old country" vernacular traditions.

Above left: The open Ark is echoed in the openness of the Ark wall.
Above right: Detail of exterior shingles.

# Chapter Eight

## Synagogue for a New Century: Creating a Stylistic Synthesis (1990–present)

This is the gateway to the LORD,
Into which the righteous shall enter

—Psalms 118:20

By 1990 Americans again were searching for an effective, meaningful synagogue style. The country entered the biggest synagogue building boom since immediately after World War II. The Jewish population was not growing, but it was moving. As the baby boom generation aged, they not only chose to live in new places, but increasingly sought to create new kinds of Jewish environments. In general, Conservative and Reform Jews have formed many newer, smaller congregations, in the pattern of Orthodox congregations. The Reconstructionist movement, positioned between the Conservative and Reform movements, has gained several hundred congregations in the past generation, which are only now beginning to build new synagogues.[1]

Congregations have striven to achieve a balance of appropriate community size with adequate resources to maintain a rabbi, staff, and small facility. For many congregations balance, not unlimited growth, is the goal. They have seen how the growth of many older congregations has not necessarily been a sign of either financial or spiritual health.

New congregations increasingly look for spaces that are adaptable. Younger rabbis and administrators recognize that religious needs will shift in time, and that to sustain a building, the building needs to be able to adapt, too. Thus, new synagogues have fewer fixed features. Seating is frequently movable, as are the *bimah* and Ark. Spaces can be changed not just in a generation, but even from week to week as a congregation seeks to include all its members by offering a variety of religious experiences—some formal, others intimate.

Modernism has not been rejected, but the gigantism of the postwar period was deemed counterproductive to the creation of a spiritually aware population. Contemporary architects adapted many of the expressive features of modernism into a more intimate language conducive to prayer, reflection, and communal bonding. Many Jews returned to urban areas and reintroduced synagogues to neighborhoods empty of Jews for generations. In some instances, Jews reclaimed and restored historic synagogues.

New congregations frequently call on architects to adaptively reuse older buildings. These include warehouses, skating rinks, churches and private houses that have been bequeathed to congregations, or are affordable to start-up minyans.

In many cases, architects aim to weave their new designs into the context of existing neighborhoods. Others have continued the experiments of the 1980s, when traditional forms were incorporated in a Post-Modern language, as at the Perlman Sanctuary in Glencoe (chapter 7), or interpreted in new ways, as in East Hampton (chapter 7).

Some congregations have explicitly tried to quote the past, as in the project of Frank/Architects for Congregation Beth Israel in Berkeley, California, which designed a new sanctuary as a close replica of the destroyed wooden synagogue from Przedborz, Poland. Others have literally incorporated elements of older buildings—sometimes windows and Arks from destroyed American synagogues, and sometimes pieces from abroad or copies of them.[2] Many more synagogue builders acknowledge the force of tradition in Jewish continuity and identity, but have preferred to adapt selected elements in new ways to create entirely new forms. Architects Alexander Gorlin and Michael Landau, though very different in their aesthetics, seek to distill the essence of traditional form into a contemporary architectural language. Fortunately for them, the architectural and artistic tradition of Judaism is so rich and varied that precedents for every sort of expressive language—subdued or ebullient, classical or modern, vernacular or imperial—can be found.

Opposite: Congregation Agudas Achim, Austin, Texas.

## Gordon Chapel at Temple Oheb Shalom
**Baltimore, Maryland**
Levin/Brown
1988



The congregation of Temple Oheb Shalom in Baltimore, designed in the early 1960s by Walter Gropius and Sheldon Leavitt, faced many of the same issues that confronted North Shore Congregation Israel in Glencoe. The process of change was more gradual, but when change came it was more complete. At Oheb Shalom a new chapel was built in 1988 for much the same reason as at Glencoe. The project also included redevelopment of the business and clergy offices and the refurbishment of the gift shop and other support spaces.[3] A decade later, however, the congregation also decided to transform the Gropius sanctuary. While they preserved many elements of the original design, their priority was to best meet the congregation's religious and liturgical needs. Both projects were the work of the Maryland-based firm of Levin/Brown, whose partner Mark Levin is a congregation member. The firm is now the most active synagogue planning and design firm in the world, with involvement in more than eighty projects.[4]

The new Gordon Chapel at Oheb Shalom in Baltimore echoes forms of the earlier building, but the structure is only half the height, so it naturally defers to the older building. On the outside, the new chapel suffers from this desire to conform. Gropius's form has lost much of its essential integrity in being shrunken. Inside, however, the architects have created a distinct identity for the chapel. Lots of wood paneling and bright stained-glass windows create a warm, even cheerful atmosphere. Flexible seating and warmer, brighter colors strikingly differentiate the space, making a preferable venue for smaller prayer services and special ceremonies. "The Gropius design was right for its time and for its congregation," said its current leader, Rabbi Berlin. "But while their children felt identified with it, they didn't feel connected."[5]

The building committee's mandate was not specific, but "we wanted a chapel so warm and intimate that if you held a wedding there, you wouldn't need flowers to liven up the space," said building committee chairman Stuart Greenebaum.[6]

The chapel, while small, has a sense of open space. The ceiling is 18 feet high, but the *bimah* is low and surprisingly deep, covering a substantial portion of the room. It is close to the congregational seating—unlike the elevated *bimah* in the main sanctuary. The chapel boasts a

Right: Exterior of chapel next to the original sanctuary. The new design reflects the old, but the arches are merely decorative.

greater sense of participation and community, and this can be augmented according to need with flexible seating. Most of the chapel is lined with oak, and warm colors are used. And again, different from the Gropius design, the *bimah* is flooded with natural light from a large skylight overhead. Ten brightly colored stained-glass windows are illuminated by natural light during the day and by artificial light at night. One of these windows represents the Gropius-designed building, set beneath the torch of Lady Liberty.

In a deliberate attempt to stay away from the assertive architecture of the earlier design, however, Levin may have produced a space that is very useful and tasteful, but not especially memorable. This doesn't particularly concern the architect, however, who believes that the treasured memories should be of the events associated with the building, not of the building itself.

Opposite: New entry hallway designed by Levin/Brown as part of remodeling of original Walter Gropius design.

Top right: Exterior of chapel next to original sanctuary. The new design reflects the old, but the arches are merely decorative, not part of the structure.

Bottom right: The chapel provides a more intimate worship space with flexible seating.

## Kol Ami Synagogue
## Scottsdale, Arizona
Will Bruder
1995

196 Kol Ami Synagogue in Scottsdale, Arizona, designed by Will Bruder, signals a new approach to synagogue design.[7] Bruder looks neither to past American sources nor to Jewish Europe for inspiration. His sources are closer to home—in the desert landscape of the Southwest, in the potential of everyday building materials, and in the quirky do-it-yourself constructivism of Frank Lloyd Wright seen at his nearby school and complex, Taliesen West, and more so, Paolo Soleri at Arcosanti, an experimental town north of Phoenix being built according to hand-craft principles and an environmental philosophy.[8] Like Arcosanti, Kol Ami remains a work in progress. Planning for the synagogue on this site began in 1992, and a first phase, which included a multipurpose hall that now serves as sanctuary and social hall, was complete by 1995. A second phase now being designed will add a sanctuary to the north.

The local desert landscape might evoke the desert tradition of ancient Judaism, as in Eisenshtat's work in El Paso (chapter 6), but Bruder's approach is radically different. Where Eisenshtat brought a Romantic emotional approach to his design, Bruder's work is grounded in sharp pragmatism. Kol Ami is closer to a postwar desert kibbutz in Israel than to Mount Sinai or some other biblical icon.

The complex contains both religious and educational facilities—it is conceived, in the words of one critic, as a "modern version of the traditional fortified village of ancient desert settlements."[9] The master plan creates a tight-knit pattern of streets and protective courtyards intended to enforce a sense of community identity. The east wall of the compound forms the principal public elevation—it undulates along the full length of the complex inspired in part, Bruder claims, by the lines of a Richard Serra sculpture.[10] The building that now serves as the sanctuary is a large, solid-looking block with sheer sides and no decoration. Inside, it is an airy space sliced with sunshine that slants in through a window on the south wall, windows behind the Ark, and windows in the roof. An Ark designed by Bruder of cherry wood projects from the east wall. Outside, a galvanized metal panel extends from the east wall and allows light to enter through narrow windows. According to Bruder, he had "designed a multipurpose room that you can worship in [but that] never became sacred. . . . There is a duality to it, the way you enter in, the way it works."[11]

Right: Interior of multi-use space that serves as sanctuary. View toward the Ark.

The walls of the sanctuary consist of blocks of sand aggregate laid in courses slightly offset, recalling the rough masonry of the Wailing Wall in Jerusalem. The irregular masonry pattern catches the bright sun, which animates the wall into patterns of light and shadow. Lightweight concertina awnings of polycarbonate sheeting face the courtyard, supported by projecting narrow metal poles. They create a zigzag pattern of shadow upon the wall. These walls extend higher than the roofs of the classrooms behind them, hiding the varied roof levels that intersect in a clever way to allow the insertion of clerestory windows by which the rooms are naturally lit. Bruder varies the classroom heights within, too, by creating a series of successively lower floors. As the children grow and move from class to class, the rooms grow taller, like the occupants. The high walls also create the feel of an old Western town, where two-story facades were frequently erected before the buildings behind them went up. This device, as well as the raw feel of so many of the materials, emphasizes Temple Kol Ami as a work in progress. But unlike many construction sites, Kol Ami will maintain this quality in years to come, even when all its phases are complete.

Left: One side of the sanctuary opens into a small enclosed desert garden.

Right: The exterior of the sanctuary, with its cast blocks slightly offset, has a projection where the Ark is set within and where light filters inside.

Opposite: The court along which the classrooms are arrayed resembles the main street of an Old West town.

EXIT

## Hampton Synagogue
## Westhampton, New York
Edward Jacobs
2000



The Hampton Synagogue, a high-profile Orthodox congregation in fashionable Westhampton, New York, has literally exploded upon the Jewish scene in the summer resort. In only a few years the congregation, headed by Rabbi Marc Schneier, has grown to 1,400 families—a huge number for any synagogue, and especially large for an Orthodox congregation. Many of these members are just summer visitors, as is the rabbi himself, but the synagogue functions year-round.

The synagogue was begun in the early 1990s when Rabbi Schneier started a summer minyan in a tent in the backyard of a rented house. In 1993 a wooded lot was purchased, and in 1994 the synagogue, constructed in under a year, was dedicated. Edward Jacobs was the architectural designer and artist for the facility. He was involved in every aspect of design and construction, much as Kenneth Triester was in Miami twenty-five years earlier (chapter 6). Jacobs strove to create a complete environment that was effective functionally, emotionally, and symbolically. He wanted:

> To discover, articulate and then express materially (as best as possible) the spiritual nature of the work at hand. I believe that both inspiration and excitement may be derived by a composition that is concurrently, traditionally proper, conceptually harmonious with the religious philosophy of the congregation, and represents a fresh and true approach to what has become standard and stagnant.[12]

From the start, Rabbi Schneier was definitive in his vision of creating an environment that would welcome a Modern Orthodox congregation that also embraces a Conservative and Reform constituency. Like the Hampton Jewish Center, this congregation is in many ways post-denominational, but its starting point is rooted in Orthodoxy rather than Reform. According to Jacobs, "People in the Hamptons come from all over the religious spectrum, and we wanted them all to feel welcome, comfortable, and most importantly inspired."[13] A small year-round Orthodox congregation easily fits in the sanctuary. In the summer the outer walls open for expanded outdoor seating.

An unusual aspect of the synagogue is its stated egalitarianism. Despite the financial support of many prominent and wealthy members of the New York and Hampton Jewish communities in funding the

Left: The sanctuary can expand outdoors in good summer weather, the time when the greatest number of worshippers attend services here.

synagogue, no mention of benefactors is found in the sanctuary itself. Instead, a separate benefactors' court is outside.

The architectural sources of the building are readily apparent. The exterior, like the Hampton Jewish Center, continues the local shingle-clad vernacular. Inside, the sanctuary is designed as a tent. This refers directly to the real tent used by the first congregants, and of course to the Tabernacle of the Israelites, and further, to the now accepted tent theme common to some modern synagogues. Here, the tent has been intermingled with other traditions—noticeably, the wooden synagogues of Central and Eastern Europe. The supports of the tent are all wood, and four tall, thin piers rise up in the center surrounding the centrally placed *bimah*. These piers recall the thin supports in the wooden synagogue of Wolpa, Poland. The *bimah* can be removed and the four supports used as a wedding canopy (*huppah*). The overall design, while conforming to Orthodox requirements, is egalitarian in its provision of space for women. The sexes are given equal halves of the sanctuary, separated by a *mechitzah* that looks more like a modern sculpture than a spatial divider. This barrier can be removed to create a central aisle for weddings and nonreligious activities.

But unlike the wooden synagogues of Poland, this Hampton example is a light and airy place. A square skylight is set over the *bimah*—directly lighting the reading of the Torah, but also allowing summer light to bathe the vault. The sanctuary is open on the north and south sides, and there are windows in many walls, including behind the Ark, as part of the overall decorative and symbolic theme.

The interior meaning is based on the giving of the Torah at Mount Sinai. The entire eastern wall is to be read as a mural of the experience. Windows and Ark area depict the mountain itself with the sky above. One looks through the multihued bronze *parochet* to the fifteen-ton Jerusalem stone Ark within. Above, the Eternal Light depicts the "Cloud of Glory." By pulling on a large hanging stone located across the *bimah*, the *parochet* rises just enough to provide access to the Torah scrolls. Jacobs summarized:

> The whole Synagogue was conceived to be a multilevel experience, allowing the viewer to focus on any particular aspect of the composition, or to look through and past, to the level beyond. Viewing the *Parochet*—Ark Cover, and windows, as the mountain mural, or looking past and through, to the "mountain within the mountain" housing the Torah scrolls in protective embrace. The windows are only complete when viewed in symphony with the sky and vegetation that lay beyond. The eternal light represents "the cloud of Glory, over the mountain." The menorahs and *mechitzah* divider act as a natural and musical foliage extending from the mountain. As we are composed of "hidden and discovered layers," so to is the Synagogue, inside and out.[14]

Above: One entrance to the synagogue is a modest door, in the local tradition.

Opposite: The sanctuary looking toward the Ark. The *mechitzah* that looks like an abstract sculpture divides the seating equally for men and women.

Opposite: Detail of *mechitzah*.

Top left: Detail of Ark with Torah scrolls.
Top right: The rabbi's chair on the *bimah*.

Bottom: Sculpted bench at outdoor benefactors' court.

**Temple Israel**
**Greenfield, Massachusetts**
Louis Goodman
1996



The design and construction of Temple Israel in Greenfield, Massachusetts, a Conservative synagogue, by architect Louis Goodman, is an example of an architect and congregation creating a new combination from disparate traditions. In this case, the Old World and the New World meet in a modest wood structure that seems both rooted in its New England colonial and rural heritage and in the *shtetl* architecture of Eastern Europe. In many ways this is a more explicit evocation of the Eastern European past than earlier synagogues that incorporated wood, such as B'nai Israel in Millburn, New Jersey, by Percival Goodman (no relation).

The exterior is clad in flush pine siding and thus fits in with the New England tradition of vernacular clapboard. The building has a recessed entry porch, announced by two columns. The deep-set windows and atypical roof geometry both contribute to geometric abstraction but are also historically rooted in Polish synagogue design. "This is a contemporary building. It recalls and extends the characteristic forms of Eastern Europe and synthesizes them with modern concepts," writes Louis Goodman.[15]

The prayer hall is surmounted by a wooden barrel vault of richly stained wood. While this, too, harks back to Eastern Europe, it is also firmly set in the American synagogue tradition. Early synagogues, such as the first Beth Elohim in Charleston, had wooden vaults, in the tradition of the Amsterdam Esnoga.[16] These were easy to build in the era of wooden ship building. Goodman commented, "By using wood throughout, we have a building that reflects the European tradition and is most appropriate to the New England setting."[17] Indeed, this synagogue has the austerity of a New England Congregationalist church or a Pennsylvania Quaker meeting house. Unlike in many Polish wooden synagogues, the wood of the ceiling is emphasized.

There is no wall or ceiling painting and no ornamental embellishment of the Ark. The main decoration is calligraphic. Like many other contemporary synagogues, the story of creation is told, subtly, through a calligraphy frieze that runs around the base of the vaulting. It quotes the sayings relating to creation as told in the Book of Genesis. Surprisingly, there is no central *bimah*—not even the hint of one. But Temple Israel is small enough, and the *bimah* is very low, so that no congregant feels left out of the service. The Ark, a simple basswood cabinet, is set in a naturally lit alcove in front of which is the *bimah*. Seating is decidedly old-fashioned, on high-ended wooden benches. A balcony reached by two stairways at the entrance end can be used for overflow seating.

Right: Exterior seen from the southeast.

יהי אור
יהי רקיע
יקוו המים
תדשא הארץ
יהי מארות

Opposite: View of *bimah* and recessed Ark.
Top: Interior view to Ark.

Bottom: View from inside, looking back at the entrance. The foyer is a simple transitional space.

אין סוף
חכמה
תפארת
הוד

## North Shore Hebrew Academy Synagogue
## Kings Point, New York

Alexander Gorlin

1999



Just as North Shore Congregation Israel and Oheb Shalom updated their facilities with the addition of small sanctuaries, so the Orthodox North Shore Hebrew Academy in Kings Point, Long Island, expanded in the 1990s as well. Here, however the impetus came from without. The local Orthodox community needed a synagogue and approached the school about including a worship space that could also serve as an auditorium in their complex, an uninspired former public school built in 1958.[18]

Alexander Gorlin was hired to build the new 175-seat prayer hall into the side of a hill, with only 18 feet of the structure to be built above ground. In addition, the sanctuary was shoehorned into the corner of two of the academy's classroom wings, and thus had to conform to the existing brick exterior. With this challenge, Gorlin reached back into Jewish history to a time when the height of synagogues was often restricted by local laws. Earlier architects had found this a challenge and had sunk their floor levels to gain additional height. Best seen in the famous Altneushul in Prague, this created a surprisingly lofty interior in what seems from the outside to be a small building and a dramatic lighting scheme with natural light filtering in only from high windows far above the congregants. Gorlin has also compared his sanctuary to some synagogues in Venice that are hidden behind blank walls.

By necessity Gorlin eschewed a vista of nature—something he has excelled at using in his villa designs. Instead, he almost ignored the exterior of the building and the outside world, creating a simple, sacred environment that turns in on itself but receives light like a vessel receives water poured from above. But unlike Thomas Beeby, who found inspiration in Venice's decorative richness, Gorlin applied the lesson of filtered Venetian light.[19]

At first glance the result seems just a well-lit, wood paneled assembly hall, sleek and airy. But into the building Gorlin has poured symbolism as well as light. He refers to the Jewish mystical tradition embodied in the Zohar, the central text of Kabala. As opposed to the reference to Kabala by Norman Jaffe in the Reform Gates of Grove Synagogue (chapter 7), where most of the congregation would be ignorant of the source, Gorlin aimed his reference at the more knowledgeable Orthodox congregation and school population. According to Kabala, the *sefirot* appeared as colored rays of light when God withdrew into himself

Left: Interior with Ark on left.

Left: Entrance.
Above: Interior, view to Ark.

after the Creation of the world. The *sefirot* flow into vessels that could not hold the light, and when they broke, human history began. Here, the synagogue is the vessel; the focal point is an Ark set beneath a recessed skylight and an aluminum and glass cube. Light falls through the cube and the Ark glows. From the rear of the sanctuary, colored light filters in from extensive clerestory windows, upon which are inscribed Hebrew texts from Genesis and the Zohar referring to creation. Light sources are also set behind sections of the sanctuary's wood paneling, so that light seems trapped in the walls.

The cube above the Ark also refers to the Holy of Holies in the Temple of Solomon, a place that is described in the Book of Kings with architectural precision as "20 cubits long, 20 wide, and 20 high." The cube at North Shore Hebrew Academy is much smaller but it still serves as a symbol of holiness. Beneath this "holy of holies" are kept the Torah scrolls, believed in Orthodox Judaism to be the word of God handed down to Moses. The cube is also practical: inset within it are triangular panels of glass that refract sound back to the congregation. In an unusually explicit symbolic sleight of hand, these panels can also be seen from the *bimah* to take the shape of a Jewish star.

Above: View to the Ark, showing clerestory windows, *mechitzah*, theaterlike seating, and simple table for the Torah reading.

## Hevreh of Southern Berkshire
## Great Barrington, Massachusetts

Michael Landau Associates
1999



Hevreh of Southern Berkshire is a new congregation, founded in Great Barrington, Massachusetts, in 1974 as a Jewish education and prayer group. The *hevreh* ("society" or "association") grew quickly to fill the religious and cultural needs of a dispersed and underserved Jewish community in western Massachusetts, and affiliated as a Reform congregation with the Union of American Hebrew Congregations in 1983. After meeting in private homes, a house was purchased in 1992, and when this was outgrown, plans were laid for a new building. Michael Landau Associates of Princeton, New Jersey, was the chosen architectural firm, and the new synagogue was dedicated in 1999.

Landau, who has renovated or designed over a dozen synagogues nationwide, followed the lead of both Norman Jaffe and Louis Goodman in creating a vernacular building that utilized local building traditions. Like Kol Ami in Scottsdale (chapter 7), this is a multipurpose space. The 21,000-square-foot complex includes a full range of social and educational facilities built as low-scale structures, sheathed in a simple clapboard siding. Thus, the synagogue presents an uninspired face to the public. There is only a hint of the sanctuary in the distinctive hipped roof rising over the introductory wings. These wings screen the sanctuary from the parking area and entrance allowing arrival in the prayer hall to be the culmination of progression through several intermediary spaces. The most important of these is the central square lobby that serves as a hub off which all the spaces branch. Offices and kitchen are to the left, classrooms and meetings rooms to the right. Directly ahead is the sanctuary, seen through a curious insertion—a dividing wall cut in the profile of a hill, like those Berkshire hills that rise behind the synagogue. An arched doorway pierces this incongruous wall, and one is led into the expansive sanctuary that echoes to some degree Temple Israel in Greenfield, Massachusetts, in the workmanship of its wooden vault. Here though it is a hipped, not a barrel, vault and the spatial thrust is dissipated rather than directed. The ceiling of smooth wooden planking sits gently like a hat over the airy interior, which, because it has no fixed seating, appears even emptier than it is.

Straight ahead but just off-center is the Ark, a dramatic sculpture by Tom Patti, that sets the Torah scroll behind glass. The entire wall to

Right: The sanctuary at twilight.

the right is also glass and opens up, as the Hampton Synagogue, to an outside patio area, giving off to tame greenery and then to the wild. The most distinctive feature of Hevreh is that this patio is truly part of the sanctuary, and on the High Holidays in the lovely New England autumn, the walls open, and half the congregation sits outside—in the open or under tents. Traditionally, on Rosh Hoshanah (the Jewish New Year) Jews partake of apples and honey. Here at Hevreh, sitting in the open air, one can smell autumn air and apples while one prays for a sweet New Year. Thus, the force of nature that many modern architects have attempted to bring into their sanctuaries is here fully captured by bringing the sanctuary out of doors.

Above and left: Behind the sanctuary is the structure to support an enclosed tent, used when the congregation is large on the Holy Days, and the sanctuary wall is opened to the outdoors.

Opposite: A wall shaped like a small mountain, similar to the Berkshire Hills, serves as a divider from the central vestibule and the sanctuary.

Opposite: View to Ark and walls that open to outdoor seating.

Left: The east window of the sanctuary, which is also used as a social hall.

Bottom left: The transparent Ark, designed by Tom Patti.

Bottom right: The Ark and sanctuary at night.

## Congregation Agudas Achim

**Austin, Texas**

Lake/Flato Architects, Inc.

2001



Agudas Achim is the oldest congregation in Austin, Texas. The Orthodox congregation was chartered in 1924 after holding services in private homes for a decade. The first synagogue was located at Seventh and San Jacinto Streets in downtown Austin beginning in 1934. In 1948 the congregation affiliated with the Conservative movement, and in 1963 built a new facility at Bull Creek Road—dedicated by Lyndon Johnson just a month after he assumed the presidency. Due to Austin's rapid economic development, the congregation has grown dramatically to over 500 families–beyond the expansion rate of similar congregations elsewhere in the country. The congregation has been able to attract a constant stream of newcomers raised in the Conservative tradition. Despite the expansion of the facilities in 1989, an entirely new synagogue was dedicated in March 2001 at the Dell Community Campus, an expansive development that also includes the Austin Jewish Community Center and the Austin Jewish Day School. The move of the Agudas Achim to the Dell campus signals a new trend in American Jewish institutions to encourage grouping to better geographically unify an increasingly dispersed community, and to foster the development of shared facilities.

The architectural firm of Lake/Flato was engaged for the project. David Lake and Tim Flato are among the leading younger architects in the Southwest, and like Will Bruder, they have made a reputation with their ability to create dynamic spaces using unusual materials and configurations that are sensitive to the region's hot, dry climate.[20] Like Norman Jaffe a decade earlier, most of the firm's work had been for residential clients. This familiarity with domestic scale—the human element in architecture—certainly appealed to the congregation.

The architects were asked to create a sacred space that would comfortably seat 1,000 congregants for High Holidays, but would be intimate enough for 350 worshipers during weekly services. The congregation wanted to avoid the mistake of the large building programs of the previous generation.

The solution for the architects was relatively easy. They designed a compact building on a central plan—following the lessons first developed three-quarters of a century earlier by Alfred Altschuler and other practitioners of the Byzantine style. At Agudas Achim, however, the square plan was developed to bring the service to the congregant. The

Left: The sanctuary combines the traditional arrangement of projecting *bimah* with an ultramodern look.

architects relied on three main organizational devices. First, they introduced a central *bimah*—something that even Conservative congregations had rarely used for a hundred years. Second, they differentiated seating on the ground level so that for smaller services only those areas surrounding the *bimah* need to be filled to create a sense on completeness and inclusion. In another sensible break with the recent past, the building is designed to support the unamplified spoken word and congregation song. Third, they reintroduced the balcony as a meaningful element in synagogue design. Not a place to exile women and not last-resort seating, the balcony at Agudas Achim, which seats 550, was brought close enough to the center of the service to offer good sight lines and a hovering sense of involvement. Formally, the balcony compresses the interior like a belt, creating a taut interior geometry.

Four concrete columns form an 80-foot square with "V" beams to shape a hexagon above. The Texas sun is diffused through a skylight in the center in the shape of a Star of David. One of the few other explicit symbolic associations is the Ark wall built of dry stacked limestone, in part to recall, like in so many other synagogues, the Jerusalem stone of the Wailing Wall.

Enclosing these extremely traditional and eminently practical solutions, the architects evoked a Polish synagogue—similar to what Davis, Brody & Wisniewski had done in the 1960s. The new sanctuary recalls the destroyed barnlike buildings of the Old Country, but at the same time it looks trend-settingly modern.

Opposite: The small chapel and cactus garden.

Above: Exterior of the main entrance to the sanctuary.

Opposite: Interior of sanctuary showing stair to balcony.

Top left: The Ark.

Top right: A view to nature in the north-east corner of the sanctuary.

# Conclusion



As the photographs in this book make clear, and as this text has attempted to demonstrate, American synagogue architecture of the past century is widely varied. The synagogues presented in this book represent only a tiny fraction of those built in the twentieth century, and an even smaller percentage of synagogues in use at one time or another during this period. At any given time since the 1920s at least 3,000 American Jewish congregations have been active—and most of these have had their own synagogue buildings.

This book shows a group of outstanding buildings that were carefully designed and planned by congregations and architects. These are modern works of religious architecture of the highest order that express a substantial, if not complete, panorama of stylistic taste and spiritual aspirations.

The range of examples could have been even broader. Hundreds of other architects have designed American synagogues, too, and many of those structures are also worthy of notice and study. Still more synagogues have been built without architects—created by local builders, or simply adapted by congregants from other structures. These buildings perpetuate older religious and vernacular forms, or they embody the most standard contemporary mass-produced designs. In addition, throughout the century, many older synagogues built as early as the 1700s, but particularly after the 1870s, have remained in use, still part of the religious landscape of America.

Across the span of one hundred years American Judaism has changed in significant ways, yet many older synagogues remain in use and stay much loved by their congregations. This is possible because, despite change, the basic tenets of the religion remain stable, and the basic values of Jewish communities have been remarkably consistent.

There are particulars that all the buildings in this book share. Even more so, seeing all these buildings grouped together, allows us to identify characteristics of American synagogues that have not, perhaps, been previously obvious. For instance, few of these buildings are really successful from the outside. American synagogue architects have only rarely successfully related their buildings to the street without falling in the trap of artificiality or bombast. Perhaps this explains, in part, why so few of these buildings have been studied before.

It is only on the interiors that most architects have found their voice. An overwhelming number of these synagogues have marvelous interior spaces, seemingly sculpted within their outer shells. One has to crack the egg to get inside—where whole worlds of space, light, and decoration are at play. In ages past, synagogues were not allowed to present themselves to the public—they often had to be, at least from the street, anonymous places. In a way this has not changed. Neither the exterior of the Wilshire Boulevard Temple of the 1920s, which is at the intersection of two streets, nor B'rith Kodesh in Rochester of the 1960s, set back from the street behind a landscaped buffer, invite the passerby to sample delights within. Yet for those that do find their way, the experience is architecturally rewarding, and perhaps for some, even spiritually so.

No change has been greater than openness, in the Reform and Conservative movements, to the increased participation of women, including their assumption of leadership roles in both the liturgical and administrative realms. And yet, despite the now common sight of women rabbis and cantors on the *bimah*, and the frequent "going up" to the Torah by women congregants, the synagogue has been altered little to accommodate this change. In the mid-twentieth century few new synagogues incorporated balconies—perhaps in reaction to the older Orthodox *shuls* where women were restricted to gallery seating. In recent decades, however, the balcony has returned—not as an area of separation, but as a way of increasing inclusive seating, close to the *bimah* and Ark.

Reform congregations now regularly include more Hebrew in the services than a century ago. More holidays are celebrated in the synagogue. More prayers are read by the bar or bat mitzvah boy or girl. In many Reform synagogues congregants wear yarmulkes (head coverings), something that was strictly forbidden even a generation ago. In the Reform, Conservative, and the newer Reconstruction movements there is more tolerance for diversity of lifestyle and worship practice. Significantly, the traditional synagogue form has been able to accommodate most of these changes, too, adapting itself more to changing aesthetic taste than to new liturgical needs.

As we enter a new century, new trends emerge. At the beginning of the last century, "decorum" was still a concept commonly invoked, as well as other phrases that signified a desire to fit in. Monumentality and civic pride were important parts of any new synagogue design. Synagogues were still urban monuments, part of tight street networks and cohesive neighborhoods.

Today, the most common buzzwords of synagogue patrons and architects are *community* and *spirituality*. There is an increased attempt to create spaces friendly to groups and conducive to participation. This can mean flexible seating, smaller scale, and more use of natural materials and good lighting. Spirituality is thought to be nearer in an intimate space conducive to quiet meditation than in an enormous space designed to produce awe. For some, spirituality also suggests something mystical, instead of the traditional, everyday Jewish way of living. Thus, we increasingly find, in synagogues of all denominations, tasteful references to the Kabala and other mystical writings and traditions. Where once it was enough to inscribe the words of the *Shema* (Hear Oh Israel, the Lord Our God, the Lord is One) and the Ten Commandments, it is not uncommon to have inscriptions refer to the *sefirot* and other attributes of the Divine.

Synagogues have been intended to invite, entice, and intimidate Jewish congregants, and to express an aura of confidence and permanence to the world of the non-Jewish majority. Synagogues have offered social, sports, and entertainment activities as a means of engaging the secular Jewish community. Conservative and especially Reform synagogues have been centers of social activism. More recently, they have offered intensive adult education programs to recapture the allegiance of parents as they strive to gain the commitment of a new generation of children.

Architects have tried to understand these needs, and most often now attempt to produce buildings that try to emphasize the friendlier aspects of religious architecture over the inspirational. In this, synagogue architects of the twentieth century have moved away from the influence of the Temple and closer to the tradition of the *shul*. Even Reform congregations have looked back to a time, real or imagined, when synagogues were more like cozy clubs, homes way from home, than places of formal relationships and forced rituals.

For the most part, the enormous sanctuaries popular in the 1920s and in the 1960s are firmly in the past. Older congregations have added smaller chapels, while newer congregations do not measure their success solely on the size of their membership. It seems that, for now, enough big sanctuaries exist. The trend now is in smaller spaces for new congregations—congregations that continue to be formed at a rapid pace because of the ongoing dispersion of the American Jewish population across the entire landscape. Jews who once were congregated in only a small number of urban centers can now be found in almost every town and city of any size.

The huge migrations of American Jews in the late twentieth century to the South and West have caused new congregations to be formed at a heretofore unimaginable rate in major cities like Atlanta, Houston, Phoenix, and San Diego. But new congregations are also springing up in western Massachusetts, in the Raleigh-Durham triangle of North Carolina, throughout Arizona, New Mexico, and Colorado, and in the Pacific Northwest. In the next generation these are the centers where the newest synagogues will be built. Already in the 1990s, as we have seen, innovative new synagogues have been built in Austin, Texas, and Scottsdale, Arizona. This trend will continue.

Throughout the century, many American Jews have opted out of the organized communal expression of religion and identity, and almost every generation of the century has faced a real or perceived threat of a declining Jewish population. The building of synagogues has responded to that threat. Throughout it all, the rate of synagogue membership among American Jews has remained remarkably constant. Perhaps in the twenty-first century some Jews may find religious community via the Internet, but most likely the synagogue will remain the constant unifier and identifier in American Jewish life.

As seen in the pages of this book, the next generations of architects have a rich legacy of forms and functional solutions on which to learn and draw, and from which, when required or inspired, to depart. While prayers will remain the same, how Jews pray, and in what setting, will continue to evolve with each generation.

# Notes



**Introduction**

1 On Harrison, see Carl Bridenbaugh, *Peter Harrison: First American Architect* (Chapel Hill, N.C., 1949).

2 Carol Herselle Krinsky, *Synagogues of Europe* (Cambridge, Mass.: MIT Press, 1985), 1.

**Chapter 1**

1 The literature on the many aspects of the Temple, its history, its ritual, and its meaning is substantial. A thorough review can be found in *Encyclopaedia Judaica*, vol. 15 (Jerusalem: Keter Publishing, 1973), 942–94. Recent interpretations of the architecture based on archaeology can be found in Meir Ben-Dov, "Herod's Mighty Temple Mount," *Biblical Archaeology Review* (Nov.–Dec. 1986), reprinted in *Archaeology and the Bible: The Best of BAR, Vol. II, Archaeology in the World of Herod, Jesus and Paul*, eds. H. Shanks and D. Cole (Washington, D.C.: Biblical Archaeology Society, 1990), 21–30; and Kathleen Ritmeyer and Leen Ritmeyer, "Reconstructing Herod's Temple Mount in Jerusalem," *Biblical Archaeology Review* (Nov.–Dec. 1989), reprinted in *Archaeology and the Bible*, eds. Shanks and Cole, 31–61.

2 On "temporal architecture," see Mitchell Schwarzer, "The Architecture of Talmud," *Journal of the Society of Architectural Historians* 60:4 (2001), 474–87. On the relation of the synagogue service to the Temple service, see Lawrence Hoffman, *Canonization of the Synagogue Service* (Notre Dame: University of Notre Dame Press, 1979), and Hayim Halevy Donin, *To Pray as a Jew: A Guide to the Prayer Book and the Synagogue Service* (New York: Basic Books, 1980).

3 See Samuel Gruber, *Synagogues* (New York: Metrobooks, 1999), for an overview of world synagogue architecture.

4 The case for the separation of men and women is made in Baruch Litvin, *The Sanctity of the Synagogue* (Hoboken, N.J.: Ktav, 1959).

5 See Samuel Gruber, "The Synagogues of Eastern Europe," *Metropolis Magazine* (June 1993), 27–31.

6 This process is documented in David Kaufman, *Shul with a Pool: The "Synagogue-Center" in American Jewish History* (Hanover, N.H.: University Press of New England, 1999).

7 The separation of the sexes is mentioned in the Talmud, but because it is not explicitly mentioned in the Bible the Reform movement abolished it. In America, however, the move away from separate seating was also pragmatic, as many congregations occupied former churches where family pews were the norm. See Jonathan D. Sarna, "The Debate over Mixed Seating in the American Synagogue," in *The American Synagogue: A Sanctuary Transformed*, ed. Jack Wertheimer (New York: Cambridge University Press, 1987), 363–94.

8 William Tachau, "The Architecture of the Synagogue," *American Jewish Year Book* 28 (1926), 174.

9 Also translated as "sculptured image" in *Tanakh: The Holy Scriptures. The JPS Translation* (Philadelphia, 1988).

10 See Joseph Gutmann, "The Second Commandment and the Image in Judaism," in *Beauty in Holiness: Studies in Jewish Culture and Ceremonial Art*, ed. Joseph Gutmann (New York: Ktav, 1970), 1–14.

**Chapter 2**

1 For a summary see Allon Gal, "American Jews: The 'German' Period 1820–1887," in *Historical Atlas of the Jewish People*, ed. Eli Barnavi (New York, 1992), 174–75; and also Hasia R. Diner, *A Time for Gathering; The Second Migration 1820–1880* (Baltimore: The Johns Hopkins University Press, 1992).

2 Now in the British Museum. It is illustrated in Hyman B. Grinstein, *The Rise of the Jewish Community of New York 1654–1860* (Philadelphia: Jewish Publication Society, 1947). The map, sketched from memory, located the synagogue in Beaver Street. On the questionable reliability of the map, and the founding of the synagogue, see Leo Hershkowitz, "The Mill Street Synagogue Reconsidered," *American Jewish Historical Quarterly* 53:4 (1964), 404–10.

3 See David de Sola Pool, *The Mill Street Synagogue of the Congregation Shearith Israel* (New York: Congregation Shearith Israel, 1930).

4 C.C. Smith, "The Rev. John Pierce's Memoirs," *Proceedings of the Massachusetts Historical Society*, 2nd ser., 19 (1905), 370–71; quoted in Rachel Wishcnitzer, *Synagogue Architecture in the United States: History and Interpretation* (Philadelphia: Jewish Publication Society, 1955), 6. Pierce, a minister from Massachusetts, went to the synagogue in 1812 and described the visit in his diary.

5 By the mid-nineteenth century, Jewish architects, including Leopold Eidlitz, Henry Fernbach, and Arnold Brunner, were increasingly chosen for synagogue commissions (Albert Kahn, Eric Mendelssohn, and Percival Goodman were at the top of the list in the twentieth century).

6 The basic reference on early American synagogues remains Wischnitzer, *Synagogue Architecture in the United States*. For the synagogues listed above, see pp. 13–42. On Beth Elohim in Charleston, see Solomon Breibart, "The Synagogues of Kahal Kadosh Beth Elohim," *South Carolina Historical Magazine*, 80:3 (1979). On Baltimore, see Israel Tabak, "The Lloyd Street Synagogue of Baltimore: A National Shrine," *American Jewish Historical Quarterly* 61 (1972), 342–52; Bernard Fishman, "Lloyd Street Synagogue's Wandering Ark: Solving Architectural Mysteries in Maryland's Oldest Synagogue," *Generations* (Fall 1989), 17–21; and Bernard Fishman, "Color and Camouflage in Baltimore's Lloyd Street Synagogue, 1845–1991," in *Maryland Historical Magazine* 90:3 (Fall 1995), 287–311.

7 See Nancy Halverson Schless, "Peter Harrison, The Touro Synagogue, and the Wren City Church," *Winterthur Portfolio* 8 (1973), 187–200.

8 See Richard G. Carrott, *The Egyptian Revival: Its Sources, Monuments, and Meaning, 1808–1858* (Berkeley: University of California Press, 1978). On Crown Street, see Rachel Wischnitzer, "Thomas U. Walter's Crown Street Synagogue 1848–9," *Journal of the Society of Architectural Historians* 8:4 (1954), 29–31.

9 See Rabbi Edgar Magnin, *The Warner Murals in the Wilshire Boulevard Temple Los Angeles, California* (Los Angeles: Wilshire Boulevard Temple, 1974).

### Chapter 3

1 On the history of Shearith Israel, see David de Sola and Tamar de Sola Pool, *An Old Faith in the New World: Portrait of Shearith Israel 1654–1954* (New York: Columbia University Press, 1955), and on Brunner's building, see Maurice Berger, "Arnold Brunner's Spanish and Portuguese Synagogue: Issues of Reform and Reaffirmation in Late Nineteenth-Century America," *Arts Magazine* 54 (Feb. 1980), 164–67.

2 Rachel Wischnitzer, *Synagogue Architecture in the United States: History and Interpretation*. (Philadelphia: Jewish Publication Society, 1955).

3 On the Frank Memorial Synagogue, see Robert Tabak, *The Frank Memorial Synagogue: Structure and Symbol* (Philadelphia: Albert Einstein Healthcare Network, 2001). A photograph of Kefar Baram is found in the 1901 *Jewish Encyclopedia* under "Synagogues," illustrating the article written by Brunner. Brunner also was inspired by a smaller synagogue in the same location and one in nearby Nabratein.

4 Arnold W. Brunner, "Synagogue Architecture," *The Brickbuilder* 16:3 (Mar. 1907), 37.

5 On the history of Temple Society of Concord, see Benjamin Friedman, "The Days of Our Years: A History of the Society of Concord," *Society of Concord: One Hundreth Anniversary 1839–1939* (Syracuse, N.Y.: Temple Society of Concord, 1939); Ezra Greenhouse, *Society of Concord: 1839–1979, A Triumph of Dedication and Faith* (Syracuse, N.Y.: Temple Society of Concord, 1979); and B.G. Rudolph, *From a Minyan to a Community: A History of the Jews of Syracuse* (Syracuse, N.Y.: Syracuse University Press, 1970).

6 Quoted in Greenhouse, *Society of Concord*.

7 See the frontispiece of W. Hawkins Ferry, *The Legacy of Albert Kahn* (Detroit: Detroit Institute of Arts, 1970).

8 The arrangement would have been known to Goodman as a plan and photos of the Texas synagogue were published in *Architectural Record* in 1939. See Bruno Funaro, "American Synagogue Design: 1729 to 1939," *Architectural Record* 86 (Nov. 1939), 58–65.

9 Between his arrival in New York from Spain in 1881 until 1962 when the firm closed, Guastavino and his son, Rafael, and their successors installed their masonry floors, ceilings, vaults, domes, stairs and acoustic products in churches, museums, railroad stations, state capitols, libraries, concert halls, government and university buildings, private homes, bridge approaches, overpasses, and tunnels. Nearly 400 works were built in New York, more than in any other city. They include the Oyster Bar in Grand Central Terminal and the Cathedral Church of St. John the Divine, where the largest Guastavino dome ever built crowns the crossing. Some, like the original Pennsylvania Station, lamentably are gone. At the turn of the century, the Guastavinos were working with a list of architects that reads like a Who's Who of American building design: McKim, Mead & White, Richard Morris Hunt, Ralph Adams Cram, Cass Gilbert, Bertram Goodhue, and others. The Guastavinos' patented vaulting techniques made it possible for these architects to create the bold, broad spaces that they would become famous for. Since he served as a contractor on these projects, the Guastavino name did not appear on the buildings, and the accomplishments of the firm remained relatively unknown to the public. By 1891 the company had offices in New York, Boston, Providence, Milwaukee and Chicago. In 1900 it opened a factory to manufacture tile in Woburn, Massachusetts. The tiles were lightweight, fireproof, and able to withstand very heavy loads.

10 On proposed meanings of columns in the Jewish artistic vocabulary, see Bracha Yaniv, "The Origins of the 'Two-column Motif' in European Parokhot," *Jewish Art* 15 (1989), 26–43.

11 See Lauren Weingarden Rader, "Synagogue Architecture in Illinois," *Faith & Form: Synagogue Architecture in Illinois. An Exhibition Organized by the Spertus Museum* (Chicago: Spertus College Press, 1976).

12 See Rader, *Faith and Form*, 49, for a photo.

13 Alfred S. Alschuler, "The Building of a Temple," *Reform Advocate* (Mar. 16, 1912), 199.

14 Ibid.

15 Temple Sholom on Pine Grove Avenue and Grace Street (now occupied by Anshe Emet) was dedicated on April 7–9, 1911. B'nai Sholom Temple Israel at 53rd Street and Michigan Avenue was built in 1914.

16 Alfred S. Alschuler, "The New Home of Congregation B'nai Sholom Temple Israel," *Reform Advocate* 42 (May 2, 1914), 371, quoted in Rader, *Faith and Form*, 52.

17 Rodef Shalom is the oldest Congregation in western Pennsylvania. The first building was erected in 1862 on Hancock Street (later Eighth Street), designed by Charles Bartberger. Within a year, the congregation became a leader of the new Reform movement. Services were shortened, the women sat with the men, and an organ was installed. By 1874, the practice of men wearing of a hat or yarmulke was abolished, and Rodef Shalom joined the Union of American Hebrew Congregations. Reform leadership was cemented when the Temple hosted a conference of Reform rabbis in 1885, who created the "Pittsburgh Platform," which guided Reform Judaism until 1937, when a different platform was adopted.

18 Hornbostel was one of America's foremost classicists. He graduated in 1891 at the head of his class at the School of Mines at Columbia University, and shortly thereafter left for Paris, where he studied at the Ecole des Beaux-Arts and worked for Charles-Louis Girault (1851–1932), a prominent practitioner of the decorative Classicism popular at the turn of the century. The style is most evident in the 1900 Paris exhibition, for which Girault designed the Petit Palais. Hornbostel arrived in Pittsburgh in 1904 as the architect of the new Carnegie Institute of Techonology, where he also founded the school of architecture and served as its first director. With William Palmer he designed the Pittsburgh City Hall (1910) and the Soldier and Sailors Memorial (1911), as well as dozens of major

buildings and monuments across the country. See Steven McLeod Bedford, "Hornbostel, Henry," in *Macmillan Encyclopedia of Architects*, ed. Adolf K. Placzek, vol. 2 (New York: Free Press, 1982), 420–21.

19 See Franklin Toker, *Pittsburgh: An Urban Portrait* (Pittsburgh: University of Pittsburgh Press, 1986), 115. Rodef Shalom did not turn to Beman for its building, despite his experience designing synagogues. He was responsible for at least two: the North Chicago Hebrew Congregation (1894–1895) and Lasalle St. Synagogue (before 1907), both in Chicago. See Rader, *Faith and Form*, 43, for the former.

20 Toker, *Pittsburgh*, 114.

21 *The American Architect and Building News* 93: 1682 (Mar. 18, 1908).

22 "One of the Most Beautiful and Costly Jewish Synagogues in the United States, Soon to be Dedicated with Impressive Ceremonies for Members of Rodeph Shalom Congregation in Pittsburgh," *Pittsburgh Post* (Sept. 1, 1907).

**Chapter 4**

1 William Tachau, "The Architecture of the Synagogue," *Architecture* (Sept. 1928), 129–44.

2 R.R. Stanwood, "Temple Tifereth Israel, Cleveland, Ohio." *Architectural Forum* 43:5 (Nov. 1925), 275; and Rachel Wischnitzer, *Synagogue Architecture in the United States: History and Interpretation* (Philadelphia: Jewish Publication Society, 1955), 110.

3 Most of Charles Greco's buildings are in the Boston area, where he was born, and where he was associated with Peabody and Stearns and other firms. In addition to the many courthouses, schools and churches he designed, he is also designed many synagogues, erected around the country. After the popular Temple in Cleveland, he designed Temple Beth Israel in West Hartford, Conn. (1933–36); Temple Emanu El in Miami Beach (with Albert Anis, 1949); and Temple Emanu-El in Worcester, Mass. (1949).

4 Alschuler graduated from the Armour Institute of Technology in 1899 and went to work for Chicago's established Jewish architect, Dankmar Adler. Alschuler began to practice with Samuel A. Treat in 1904, and on his own in 1908. He quickly established himself as an innovative and prolific designer of Chicago synagogues, and as a successful commercial architect. In addition to synagogues, he designed may high-rise office and commercial structures in Chicago and elsewhere. He is perhaps best known in this area for the classical London Guarantee and Accident Building (1922–23) and Chicago Mercantile Exchange (1927), and the more modern Benson & Rixon Building (1937).

Temple Isaiah was built for Isaiah Israel, the city's second Jewish congregation, which was founded in 1852. In 1971, Temple Isaiah merged with Kehilath Anshe Maariv (KAM), founded in 1847 and Chicago's oldest congregation, creating KAM Isaiah Israel Temple. Alschuler's Temple Isaiah replaced the congregation's previous home, designed by Dankmar Adler in 1898–99, at 45th and Vincennes. In this building, completed just a year before his death, Adler adapted somewhat to the new Classical taste.

5 Alfred S. Alschuler, "Isaiah Temple, Chicago, Ill.," *American Architect & The Architectural Review* 126 (Dec. 31, 1924), 624.

6 Ibid., 623.

7 "The Passing Show: Temple Isaiah," *The Western Architect* (Apr. 1927), 65–66.

8 "The Architecture of the Jews," *The Western Architect* (June 1925), 64–65.

9 Alschuler was inspired by the synagogue at Essen, Germany, designed by Edmund Körner (1875–1927) in 1911–13. The building was well known and well published during Alschuler's formative years. See Carol Herselle Krinsky, *Synagogues of Europe* (Cambridge, Mass.: MIT Press, 1985), 285–88, for a description and bibliography.

10 Alschuler believed that the Guastavino system was a "true masonry construction based soundly on Byzantine engineering principles." Alschuler, *American Architect* 126, 624.

11 "In some synagogues the star was used in reckless numbers. Many a youngster waiting for the cantor to complete the repetition of the festival *amidah* prayers spent his time counting the stars on the ark, its curtains, the synagogue walls, pew ends and fixtures, anticipating that with every counting a new star, or even a constellation of stars might be discovered." Rabbi Alexander S. Kline, "Contemporary Development in American Synagogue Art," *CCAR Journal of the Union of American Hebrew Congregation* (Oct. 1956).

12 Allison and Allison were architects of several notable religious buildings in Los Angeles including the Thirteenth Church of Christ, Scientist (1926) the First Congregational Church (1930–32), and the First Unitarian Church (1930). The firm also specialized in school buildings, including many at UCLA such as Royce Hall and Kerkoff Hall, built in the same years as the Wilshire Boulevard Temple.

13 Dianne Morris, "Wilshire Boulevard Temple and the Golden Age of Hollywood," paper presented at "The 'Church' and the City: A Conference on the Aesthetic, Architectural, Historic, and Social Impacts and Contributions of Religious Institutions on American Urban Life," Cleveland State University, Cleveland, Ohio (Apr. 18–19, 1997).

14 The synagogue is illustrated in Abraham Karp, ed., *The Jews in America: A Treasury of Art and Literature* (New York: Hugh Lauter Levin Associates, 1994), 214–15.

15 The building is also discussed in Wischnitzer, *Synagogue Architecture in the United States*, 114–16.

16 Edgar F. Magnin, *The Warner Murals in the Wilshire Boulevard Temple Los Angeles, California* (Los Angeles: Wilshire Boulevard Temple, 1974), 15 (pages unnumbered).

17 Ibid.

18 William M. Kramer, "Hugo Ballin, A Forgotten Artist of Hollywood—Part I," *Western States Jewish History* 24:1 (1991), 3–16.

19 On Boston's Temple Israel, see David Kaufman, "Temples in the American Athens: A History of the Synagogues of Boston," in *The Jews of Boston: Essays on the Occasion of the Centenary (1895–1995) of the Combined Jewish Philanthropies of Greater Boston*, eds. Jonathan D. Sarna and Ellen Smith (Boston: Combined Jewish Philanthropies of Greater Boston, 1995). Also see Anndee Hochman, *Rodeph Shalom: Two Centuries of Seeking Peace* (Philadelphia, 1995).

20 Norton, for example, one of the designers of the Wilshire Boulevard Temple, worked with S. Charles Lee on the extremely ornate Los Angeles Theater at 615 South Broadway, opened in 1931 for the premiere of Charlie Chaplin's film *City Lights*.

21 The building was designed by Eidlitz and Henry Fernbach, both born in Europe, and among the first successful Jewish architects in America. The building and contemporary synagogues are described in Robert A.M. Stern, Thomas Mellins, and David Fishman, *New York 1880* (New York: Monacelli Press, 1999), 323–33. On the early history of the congregation and its buildings also see Ronal B. Sobel, "The Congregation: A Historical Perspective," in *A Temple Treasury: The Judaica Collection of Congregation Emanu-El of the City of New York* (New York: Hudson Hills Press, 1989).

22 Robert A.M. Stern, Gregory Gilmartin, and Thomas Mellins, *New York 1930* (New York: Rizzoli, 1987), 161.

23 See Wischnitzer, *Synagogue Architecture in the United States*, 125–31; and Stern et al., *New York 1930*, 160–62, 775. For accounts at the time of construction, see "Trustees Approve Plans for New Temple Emanu-El Group: Synagogue Chapel and Community House to be Erected on Site of John Jacob Astor Mansion at 5th Avenue and 65th Street at Cost of $2,500,000," *Real Estate Record and Guide* 119 (Apr. 2, 1927), 9, 18; "Temple Emanu-El, New York City," *Architecture and Building* 61 (Oct. 1929), 297–301; Eugene N. Stern, "The Structural Frame of the New Temple Emanu-El Building," *Architectural Forum* 49 (July 1928), 111–16; Charles Butler, "The Temple Emanu-El, New York," *Architectural Forum* 42 (Feb. 1930), 151–54.

24 Clarence S. Stein, "The Problem of the Temple and Its Solution," *Architectural Forum* 52 (Feb. 1930), 155–211.

25 *Description of the New Buildings . . . Consisting of Temple Emanu-el, Beth-El Chapel and Community House*, n.d., quoted in Wischnitzer, *Synagogue Architecture in the United States*, 125.

26 See Jacob Monsky, *Within the Gates: A Religious, Social and Cultural History 1837–1962* (New York: Congregation Shaare Zedek, 1964).

27 See Melissa Faye Greene, *The Temple Bombing* (Reading, Mass.: Addison-Wesley, 1996).

28 For more on Shutze's career, see Elizabeth Meredith Dowling, *American Classicist: The Architecture of Philip Trammel Shutze* (New York: Rizzoli, 1989).

29 Mordecai M. Kaplan, "The Future of Judaism," *The Menorah Hournal* (June 1916), 160–72. For a full discussion of the development of the synagogue center, see David Kaufman, *Shul with a Pool: The Synagogue Center in American Jewish History* (Hanover, N.H.: University Press of New England, 1999).

30 Tachau, "The Architecture of the Synagogue," 143.

31 Ibid.

**Chapter 5**

1 Bruno Funaro, "American Synagogue Design 1729–1939," *Architectural Record* 86 (Nov. 1939), 58–65.

2 See George M. Goodwin, "The Design of a Modern Synagogue: Percival Goodman's Beth-El in Providence, Rhode Island," *American Jewish Archives* 44 (Spring-Summer 1993), 38ff.

3 Illustrated in Rachel Wischnitzer, *Synagogue Architecture in the United States* (Philadelphia: Jewish Publication Society, 1955), 106. Hobart was the grandson of Richard Upjohn (1802–1878), architect of New York's Trinity Church and the most outstanding ecclesiastical architect in America during the nineteenth century; he was also the son of the architect Richard Michell Upjohn (1828–1903).

4 "California Synagogue in Mission Tradition," *Architectural Record* 100 (Oct. 1946), 104.

5 Maria and Kazimier Piechotka, *Wooden Synagogues* (Warsaw, Poland: Arkady, 1959).

6 "The Last Work of a Great Architect," *Architectural Forum* (Feb. 1955), 106–15.

7 Quoted in Richard Meier, *Recent American Synagogue Architecture* (New York: The Jewish Museum, 1963), 24.

8 Eric Mendelsohn, "In the Spirit of our Age," *Commentary* 3 (1947), 541.

9 These are profusely illustrated in Bruno Zevi, *Erich Mendelsohn Opera Completa; Architetture e Immagini Architettoniche* (Milan: ETAs/KOMPASS, 1970), 303ff.

10 The history of the B'nai Amoona project is described in detail in Hans R. Morganthaler, "'It will be hard for us to find a home': Projects in the United States 1941–1953," in *Eric Mendelsohn Architect 1887–1953*, ed. Regina Stephan (New York: Monacelli Press, 2000), 243–45.

11 Armand Cohen, "Eric Mendelsohn as a Man and Friend," *The Reconstructionist* 20 (Oct. 29, 1954), 16, quoted in Morganthaler, ibid., 248.

12 Cohen, ibid..

13 These designs can be seen in Zevi, *Erich Mendelsohn Opera Completa*, and as they were sometimes completed by others in "The Last Work of a Great Architect" *Architectural Forum* (Feb. 1955), 106–15.

14 On Goodman's career, see Kimberly J. Elman and Angela Giral, eds., *Percival Goodman: Architect, Planner, Teacher, Painter* (New York: Miriam and Ira D. Wallach Gallery, Columbia University, 2001). See also Evelyn Greenberg, "The Tabernacle in the Wilderness: The *Mishkan* Theme in Percival Goodman's Modern American Synagogues," *Jewish Art* 19–20 (1993–94), 44–55.

15 The essence of the symposium was published several years later as Peter Blake, *American Synagogue for Today and Tomorrow* (New York: Union of American Hebrew Congregation, 1956). See also George Goodwin, "The Design of a Modern Synagogue: Percival Goodman's Beth-El in Providence, Rhode Island," *American Jewish Archives* 44 (1993), 31–71, esp. 44ff.

16 Percival Goodman and Paul Goodman, "Tradition and Function," *Commentary* (June 1947), 542–44. This was followed a year and a half later with "Modern Artist as Synagogue Builder: Satisfying the Needs of Today's Congregation," also by Percival Goodman and Paul Goodman, in *Commentary* (Jan. 1949), 51–55.

17 Like Mendelson, Fritz Nathan (1891–1960) was a Jewish refugee architect. In the 1950s he built several influential modern synagogues: Sons of Israel in Woodmere, Long Island, (1948–50), with Eugene Schoen; Torah Israel Sephardic Society of Sheepshead Bay, Brooklyn (design), (1953); Jewish Community Center, White Plains, N.Y. (1957); and Temple Mishkin Israel, Hamden, Conn. (1960). Nathan's work was more coolly austere than Mendelsohn's, but some of Goodman's work relates to it.

18 George Goodwin, "The Design of a Modern Synagogue," 31–71.

19 See Avram Kampf, *Contemporary Synagogue Art: Developments in the United States, 1945–1965* (Philadephia: Jewish Publication Society of America, 1966), 75–86. Goodman addressed the subject of integrating art into the synagogue in Percival Goodman, "Worship and the Arts in the Jewish Tradition," *Architectural Record* 118 (Dec. 1955), 170–71. See also "Vigorous Art in the Temple," *Architectural Forum* 110 (May 1959), 140–45.

20 By 1956 there were scores of examples of synagogue art from around the country, many of which were described in Rabbi Alexander S. Kline, "Contemporary Development in American Synagogue Art," *CCAR Journal of the Union of American Hebrew Congregation* (Oct. 1956). According to Kline, "Today, new temples, regardless of their size and the limitations placed on their construction cost, include plans for artistic interpretation of aspects of the teachings and traditions of Judaism."

21 George Goodwin, "The Design of a Modern Synagogue," 55.

22 The inscriptions mostly are from the portion of Genesis describing Jacob's dream of a ladder to heaven, and his naming the place "Beth El."

23 Alexander S. Kline, "Contemporary Development in American Synagogue Art," 4.

24 Quoted in "Frank Lloyd Wright: a Special Portfolio," *Architectural Forum* (June 1959), 115–45. Also cited in Mortimer J. Cohen, *Beth Sholom Synagogue: Description and Interpretation* (Elkins Park, Penn.: Beth Sholom Synagogue, 1959), 2. The working relationship between Wright and Rabbi Cohen, and the history of the project is described in detail in George M. Goodwin, "Wright's Beth Sholom Synagogue," *American Jewish History* 86:3 (1998), 325–48.

25 "Frank Lloyd Wright: A Special Portfolio," *Architectural Forum* (June 1959), 115–45.

26 Yukio Futagawa, ed., *F.L. Wright Monograph*, vol. 8 (Tokyo: A.D.A. Edita, 1988).

27 Mortimer J. Cohen, *Beth Sholom Synagogue: A Description and Interpretation* (Elkins Park, Penn., 1959).

28 Ibid.

29 Quoted in Meier, *Recent American Synagogue Architecture*, 8.

30 Kampf, *Contemporary Synagogue Art*, 31–32.

31 Zevi, "Hebraism and the Concept of Space-Time in Art," 155.

32 The congregation was first formed as Congregation Kneses Israel (assembly of Israel) in 1887. A splinter group formed Congregation Tifereth Israel (glory of Israel) in 1903. The two congregations merged in 1927. For a history of the congregations, see *A Century of Jewish Commitment 1887–1987: Congregation Kneses Tifereth Israel* (Port Chester, N.Y., 1987).

33 See Franz Schulze, *Philip Johnson; Life and Work* (New York: Alfred A. Knopf, 1994), 238–40.

34 Meier, *Recent Synagogue Architecture*, 22.

35 Kampf first referred to it as "monumental jewel box." See Kampf, *Contemporary Synagogue Art*, 34.

36 Letter from Philip Johnson to Marjorie Tunick (May 21, 1986), in the files of Congregation Kneses Tifereth Israel.

37 We do not know whether Johnson knew of this tradition, though information on these buildings, including plans, had been published in German (which Johnson knew) and in English.

38 "Synagogue at Port Chester, U.S.A.," *Architect and Building News* 218 (Dec. 1960), 821–22.

39 See Nancy Gale Heller, "The Sculpture of Ibram Lassaw" (unpublished Ph.D. diss., Rutgers University, 1982), and Ibram Lassaw, *Space Explorations: A Retrospective Survey, 1929–1988* (Easthampton, N.Y.: Guild Hall Museum, 14 Aug.–25 Sept. 1988). Lassow also created synagogue art for Temple Beth El in Springfield, Massachusetts, designed by Percival Goodman. Here his menorah and eternal light are much less assertive. They are essentially wire sculptures made of welded metal rods. They are transparent and appear to float in a sanctuary that is warmer and more engaging than the Congegration Kneses Tifereth Israel. These works are illustrated in Kampf, *Contemporary Synagogue Art*, 199–201.

40 Kampf, *Contemporary Synagogue Art*, 193.

41 Letter from Ibram Lassaw to Majorie Tunick (July 2, 1986), in the archives of Congregation Kneses Tifereth Israel, Port Chester, New York.

**Chapter 6**

1 Lawrence Hoffman, "Why Congregations Need to Change," *Reform Judaism* 28:4 (Summer 2000), 49–50.

2 The iconography of the window is discussed in Avram Kampf, *Contemporary Synagogue Art: Developments in the United States 1945–1965* (Philadelphia: Jewish Publication Society of America, 1966), 256–59.

3 See Lauren Weingarden Rader, "Synagogue Architecture in Illinois," *Faith and Form: Synagogue Architecture in Illinois. An Exhibiton Organized by the Spertus Museum* (Chicago: Spertus College Press, 1976), 68–69.

4 See Lauren Weingarden Rader, "Synagogue Architecture in Illinois," 79 n.68.

5 Among some of the most noteworthy are the "Fire" and "Water" installations at Temple Emanu-El in San Francisco designed by Mark Adams and made by George McKeever. These windows, which are in the west and east sanctuary walls are each composed of seven levels of segments set within the stone tracery of the

large arched thermal windows. Each window is fashioned from 2,000 pieces of glass of more than 200 colors. See Abraham J. Karp, ed., *The Jews in America: A Treasury of Art and Literature* (New York: Hugh Lauter Levin Associates, 1994), 263.

6 See Marion Dean Ross, "Pietro Belluschi," in *Macmillan Encyclopedia of Architects*, vol. 1, 172–73.

7 Meredith L. Clausen, *Spritual Space: The Religious Architecture of Pietro Belluschi* (Seattle: University of Washington Press, 1992), 108. Clausen's study presents all of Belluschi's religious commissions, including his five synagogues: Temple Israel, Swampscott, Mass. (1953–56); Temple Adath Israel, Merion, Penn. (1956–59); Temple B'rith Kodesh, Rochester, N.Y. (1959–63); Temple B'nai Jeshurun, Short Hills, N.J. (1964–68) with Kelly & Gruzen; and United Hebrew Congregation, St. Louis, Mo. (1986–89).

8 Richard Meier, *Recent Synagogue Architecture* (New York: The Jewish Museum, 1963), 19.

9 Author's interview with Luise Kaish, June 20, 2002.

10 On the early history of Oheb Shalom, see William Rosenae, *A Brief History of Congregation Oheb Shalom* (Baltimore: Guggenheimer, Weil & Co., 1903); and Louis F. Cohn, *History of Oheb Shalom 1853–1953* (Baltimore: Oheb Shalom Congregation, 1953). See also Earl Pruce, *Synagogues, Temples, and Congregations of Maryland: 1830–1990* (Baltimore: Jewish Historical Society of Maryland, 1993).

11 http://www.templeohebshalom.org/history.htm (May 21, 2002).

12 In 2001 Levin/Brown completed a reconfiguration of the original sanctuary. The uphill orientation of the sanctuary was reversed, and the entire space reduced by turning the *bimah* area into a separate lecture hall that could still be opened to the sanctuary to provide more holiday seating. The old social hall was entirely refurbished and divided into new space to provide more options for meeting rooms. The entrance lobby was also redesigned. Based on materials provided by Levin/Brown & Associates.

13 Quoted by Jareene W. Barkdoll, in *United States Department of the Interior, National Park Service, National Register of Historic Places Registration Form: Temple Oheb Shalom synagogue* (Dec. 6, 1992), sec. 8, p. 4.

14 "A Big Temple for Baltimore," *Architectural Record* (June 1964), 147.

15 Ibid.

16 Jareene W. Barkdoll, *National Register of Historic Places Registration Form*, sec. 7, p. 2.

17 "A Big Temple for Baltimore," *Architectural Record* (June 1964), 149.

18 Illustrated in Kampf, *Contemporary Synagogue Art*, 66.

19 Ibid., 68.

20 A history of the congregation can be found at http://www.nsci.org/history.html.

21 Forty families voted on the idea and a spiritual leader, Rabbi Emil G. Hirsch of Sinai Congregation, was asked to be the "traveling" rabbi. Because of his prior commitments, services were held on Friday nights. On June 1, 1920, the first services were held at the Hubbard Woods School in Winnetka, Illinois. Services were held at irregular intervals, whenever a rabbi was available.

In 1924 the congregation affiliated itself with the Union of American Hebrew Congregations, reporting a membership of 198 families, all residents of the North Shore. Worship was held at the Winnetka Congregational Church, but there was soon support for a permanent house of worship. On April 19, 1926, the members voted that the congregation should become independent of Sinai Congregation. The site in Glencoe was selected and in June the name North Shore Congregation Israel was chosen.

22 Minoru Yamasaki, *A Life in Architecture* (New York: Weatherhill, 1979), 81.

23 The architect quoted in "A Synagogue by Yamasaki," *Architectural Record* 135 (Sept. 1964), 192.

24 See Rachel Wischnitzer, *Synagogue Architecture in the United States: History and Interpretation*. (Philadelphia: Jewish Publication Society, 1955). 172. Also see "A Tentlike Helix Spirals up to Create a Temple Sanctuary," *Architectural Record* 146:1 (July 1969), 119–22.

25 See "Temple's Slanting Walls Create an upwardly Directed Symbolic Form," *Architectural Record* (Mar. 1968), 133. Max Abramovitz worked in partnership with Wallace Harrison for most of his career, but the architects took credit for buildings they individually designed. Harrison's work is treated in Victoria Newhouse, *Wallace K. Harrison, Architect* (New York: Rizzoli, 1989). Abramovitz, often a highly innovative designer, has not yet received the study he deserves.

26 Hallelujah.
Praise God in His sanctuary;
praise Him in the sky , His stronghold.
Praise Him for His mighty acts;
praise Him for His exceeding greatness.
Praise Him with blasts of the horn;
praise Him with harp and lyre.
Praise Him with timbrel and dance;
praise Him with lute and pipe.
Praise Him with resounding cymbals;
praise Him with loud-clashing cymbals.
Let all that breathes praise the Lord.
Hallelujah.

27 Quoted in Richard Meier, *Recent Synagogue Architecture*, 19.

28 Quoted in "The Old Tradition," *Progressive Architecture* (Mar. 1965), 138. On this synagogue, see also Evelyn Greenberg, "Sanctity in the Woodwork," *Hadassah Magazine* (Oct. 1996), 29.

29 Quoted in "The Old Tradition," *Progressive Architecture* (Mar. 1965), 140.

30 Ibid.

31 See "Synagogue Design: Forging an Aesthetic Unbound by Tradition," *Progressive Architecture* (Mar. 1966), 146–50.

32 The synagogue has not previously been published, but see the booklet *Dedication Temple Brith Sholom, Cortland, New York (Sunday, September 7, 1969)*, and Raphael Seligmann, "A Tribute to Werner Seligmann: A Son's Fond Memories of his Dad," in *Temple Brith Sholom: A Special, First, Commemorative Issue* (Sept. 2,

1999). I would like to thank Mrs. Jean Seligmann for these materials and for her sharing her knowledge of the synagogue's history and architecture.

33 On the design of the chapel, see Kenneth Treister, *Chapel of Light: Jewish Ceremonial art in the Sophie & Nathan Gumenick Chapel* (New York: Union of American Hebrew Congregations, 2001).

34 Kenneth Treister, *Chapel of Light*, 18.

35 Ibid., 19.

**Chapter 7**

1 This is particularly evident in Philadelphia where both the Center City Synagogue and Congregation Kesher Israel (both founded in the previous century in former churches) were revived and restored by the influx into the gentrified Society Hill neighborhood of young Jews, many relocating to where their grandparents had first settled.

2 See *Religious buildings/by the editors of Architectural Record (*New York: Architectural Record, 1979), 14–18.

3 Bartos was born in New York in 1910, obtained his master's degree in architecture from MIT in 1935, and served in the U.S. Navy during the war before opening his own firm in New York. Among his other notable buildings in a Jewish context is the library of Yeshiva University.

4 Golub's work, often brightly colored abstract fabric design for torah mantles, Ark curtains, and other synagogue fittings, have been commissioned by more than twenty American congregations. For a listing, see http://www.inagolub.com/commissions.html.

5 See "Historicist Addition to a '60s Temple: North Shore Congregation Israel Addition, Glencoe, Ill.," *Architecture* (May 1984), 208–11.

6 Quoted in Charles K. Gandee, "Tradition Rekindled," *Architectural Record* (June 1983), 106.

7 Ibid.

8 Peter L. Rothholz, "Renaissance Rabbi: David J. Gelfand Brings Aspen to The Jewish Center of the Hamptons," *Long Island Jewish World* 30:22 (June 8–14, 2001).

9 Carol Herselle Krinsky, "Gates of the Grove Synagogue: A New Space Encloses the Past, Present and Future," *Journal of the Interfaith Forum on Religion, Art & Architecture* (Winter 1989–90), 47.

10 Quoted in Andrea Oppenheimer Dean, "The Beauty of Holiness," *Architecture* 78:12 (Dec. 1989), 72.

11 Jaffe was inclined to a level of mysticism well beyond the norms of American Judaism. He sought spiritual sustenance in the mountains of India, and in eastern religions.

12 Quoted in Andrea Oppenheimer Dean, "The Beauty of Holiness," 72.

13 Peter L. Rothholz, "Renaissance Rabbi," *Jewish Sentinel* 30:22 (June 8–14, 2001).

**Chapter 8**

1 On the rise of the Reconstructionist movement, the youngest of the four branches of American Judaism, see Reena Sigman Friedman, *The Emergence of Reconstructionism: An Evolving American Judaism, 1922–1945*, online at http://huc.edu/aja/Fried.htm. Reconstructionists see Judaism as an evolving religion in which the "the past has a vote, not a veto"; see "Who is a Reconstructionist Jew?" at http://www.jrf.org/recon/whois.html. There is no distinctive Reconsturctionist synagogue type, and functionally, their buildings closely resemble Conservative and Reform synagogues.

2 This project, still in progress at the time of this writing, can be viewed at http://www.wooden synagogue.org/index.html.

3 Erika Rosenfeld, "The New Intimate Sanctuary," *Reform Judaism* (Fall 1994), 39.

4 Adam Stone, "Designs on Spirituality," *Baltimore Jewish Times* (Aug. 3, 2001), cover story.

5 Quoted in Rosenfeld, "The New Intimate Sanctuary," 39.

6 Ibid.

7 Abby Bussel, "Will Power," *Progressive Architecture* (July 1995), 86; Phoebe Chow, "Elemental Abstraction," *Architectural Review* 202:1209 (Nov. 1997), 54–57.

8 Bruder is a self-trained architect who worked with Soleri, William Wenzel, and Gunnar Birkets. He sits on the Board of the Cosanti Foundation, which oversees Arcosanti. For more on Arcosanti, see Paul Heyer, *Architects of Architecture* (New York: Walker and Company, 1966), 79. When complete, Arcosanti will "house 7,000 people, demonstrating ways to improve urban conditions and lessen our destructive impact on the earth" (http://www.arcosanti.org).

9 Chow, "Elemental Abstraction," 54

10 Author interview with Will Bruder, Oct. 22, 2002.

11 Ibid.

12 Email interview with Edward Jacobs, Oct. 22, 2002.

13 Ibid.

14 Ibid.

15 Evelyn L. Greenberg, "Sanctity in the Woodwork," *Hadassah Magazine* (Oct. 1996), 29–32.

16 See Rachel Wischnitzer, *Synagogue Architecture in the United States: History and Interpretation* (Philadelphia: Jewish Publication Society, 1955).

17 Quoted in Greenberg, "Sanctity in the Woodwork," 31.

18 See Henry Urbach, "Vessel of Light." *Interior Design*, 70:9 (July 1999), 118–123.

19 Gorlin, like Philip Trammell Shutze (chapter 3) and Luise Kaish (chapter 6), is a Fellow of the American Academy in Rome and has drawn on his Italian experience in his architecture.

20 See *Lake/Flato* (Rockport, Me.: Rockport Publishers, 1996).

# Bibliography


Abramovitz, Max. "Synagogue." In *Forms and Functions of Twentieth Century Architecture*, vol. 3, ed. Talbot Hamlin. New York, Columbia University Press, 1952.

Agam, Yaacov. "My Ideal Synagogue." *Reform Judaism* (Fall 1994), 44–46.

"Agudath Shalom Synagogue." *P/A* (Mar. 1966), 154–88.

Alschuler, Alfred S. "Isaiah Temple, Chicago." *American Architect & The Architectural Review* (Dec. 31, 1924), 623–26.

———. "The New Home of Congregation B'nai Sholom Temple Israel." *Reform Advocate* (May 2, 1914), 371–413.

Armstrong, Foster, Richard Klein, and Cara Armstrong. *A Guide to Cleveland's Sacred Landmarks*. Kent, Oh.: Kent State University Press, 1992.

Berger, Maurice. "Arnold Brunner's Spanish and Portuguese Synagogue: Issues of Reform and Reaffirmation in Late Nineteenth-Century America." *Arts Magazine* 54 (Feb. 1980), 164–67.

Bernstein, Gerald. "Two Centuries of American Synagogue Architecture." In *Two Hundred Years of American Synagogue Architecture*. Waltham, Mass.: Brandeis University, Rose Art Museum, 1976.

"Beth Zion Temple, Buffalo, New York." *Architectural Record* 143 (Mar. 1968), 133–36.

"A Big Temple for Baltimore." *Architectural Record* (June 1964), 147–52.

Black, L. Perlis. *Synagogue Architecture and Planning: An Annotated Bibliography*. Monticello, Ill.: Vance Bibliographies, #1469, Feb. 1978.

Blake, Peter, ed. *An American Synagogue for Today and Tomorrow: A Guidebook to Synagogue Design and Construction*. New York: UAHC, 1954.

"B'rith Kodesh, Rochester, New York." *Architectural Record* 133 (Nov. 1963), 143–48.

Brunner, Arnold W. "Synagogue Architecture." In *The Jewish Encyclopedia*. New York and London: Funk & Wagnalls Company, 1905.

———. "Synagogue Architecture." *The Brickbuilder,* part I, 16:2 (Feb. 1907), 20–25; part II, 16:3 (Mar. 1907), 37–43 and plates.

Bussel, Abby. "Will Power." *Progressive Architecture* (July 1995), 86.

Butler, Charles. "The Temple Emanu-El, New York." *Architectural Forum* 42:2 (Feb. 1930), 151–54.

Carrott, Richard G. *The Egyptian Revival: Its Sources Monuments and Meaning, 1808–1858*. Berkeley: University of California Press, 1978.

Chevlowe, Susan, ed. *Common Man, Mythic Vision: The Paintings of Ben Shahn*. New York and Princeton, N.J.: The Jewish Museum and Princeton University Press, 1999.

Chow, Phoebe. "Elemental Abstraction." *Architectural Review* 202:1209 (Nov. 1997), 54–57.

Clausen, Meredith. *Spiritual Space: The Religious Architecture of Pietro Belluschi*. Seattle: University of Washington Press, 1992.

Crosbie, Michael J. *Architecture for the Gods*. New York: Watson-Guptill Publishers, 2000.

Currik, Max C. "A Visitor's Report on the Wilshire Boulevard Temple, Los Angeles, and on the Architecture of Temple Emanu-El, San Francisco, in 1937." *Western States Jewish Historical Quarterly* 13:1 (1980), 49–52.

Davis, Patricia Talbot. *Together They Built a Mountain*. Lititz, Penn.: Sutter House, 1974.

Dean, Andrea Oppenheimer. "The Beauty of Holiness: Gates of Grove Synagogue." *Architecture* 28:12 (Dec. 1989), 68–73.

"Dedication of New Isaiah Temple." *Reform Advocate* (Sept. 13, 1924), 200–201.

Dowling, Elizabeth Meredith. *American Classicist: the Architecture of Phillip Trammel Shutze*. New York: Rizzoli International Publications, 1989.

Eckert, Kathryn Bishop. *Buildings of Michigan*. New York: Oxford University Press, 1993.

Elman, Kimberly, and Angela Giral, eds. *Percival Goodman: architect, planner, teacher, painter.* New York: Columbia University, Miriam and Ira D. Wallach Art Gallery, 2001.

Elstein, Rochelle Berger. "Synagogue Architecture in Michigan and the Midwest: Material Culture and the Dynamics of Jewish Accomodation, 1865–1945." Ph.D. diss., Michigan State University, 1986.

Fattal, Laura Rachel Felleman. "American Sephardi Synagogue Architecture." *Jewish Art* 19–20 (1993–94), 22–43.

Fischler, Marcelle S. "The Jewish Center of the Hamptons." *New York Times* (May 21, 2000).

Freelander, Daniel Hillel. "Why Temples Look the Way They Do." *Reform Judaism* (Fall 1994).

Fumaro, Bruno, 1939. "American Synagogue Design: 1729–1939." *Architectural Record* 86 (Nov. 1939), 58–65.

Futagawa, Yukio, ed. *Frank Lloyd Wright Monograph*. Tokyo, 1988.

Gandee, Charles, K. "Tradition Rekindled." *Architectural Record* (June 1983), 104–113.

Garey, C.C. "Architectural landmarks: [synagogues]." *House Beautiful* (Dec. 1985), 11.

George, Paul S. "Temples in the Sun: Dade County's Historic Synagogues." *Preservation Today* (Fall 1992), 7–11.

Goodman, Percival. "The Essence of Designing a Synagogue." *Faith & Form* (1967), 16–17.

———. "Modem Artists as Synagogue Builders." *Commentary* 7:1 (Jan. 1949), 51–55.

———. "Worship and the Arts in the Jewish Tradition." *Architectural Record* 118 (Dec. 1955), 170–71.

Goodwin, George M. "The Design of a Modern Synagogue: Percival Goodman's Beth-El in Providence, Rhode Island." *American Jewish Archives* 44 (Spring–Summer 1993), 31–71.

———. "Wright's Beth Sholom Synagogue." *American Jewish History* 86:3 (1998), 325–48.

Gordis, Robert. "Seating in the Synagogue—Minhag America." *Judaism* 141:36 (Winter 1987), 47–53.

Gordon, Albert I. *Jews in Suburbia*. Boston: Beacon Press, 1959.

Gordon, Mark. "Rediscovering Jewish Infrastructure: Update on United States Nineteenth

Century Synagogues." *American Jewish History* 75:3 (Mar. 1996), 11–27.

Greenberg, Evelyn. "Sanctity in the Woodwork." *Hadassah Magazine* (Oct. 1996), 29–32.

Gruber, Samuel. *Synagogues*. New York: Metrobooks, 1999.

Gutstein, M.A. *A Priceless Heritage: The Epic Growth of Nineteenth Century Chicago Jewry*. New York, 1953.

Hardin, Evamaria. *Syracuse Landmarks: An AIA Guide to Downtown and Historic Neighborhoods*. Syracuse, N.Y.: Syracuse University Press, 1993.

Hayes, Barlett. *Tradition Becomes Innovation: Modern Religious Architecture in America.* New York: Pilgrim Press, 1983.

Heilman, Samuel C. *Synagogue Life: A Study in Symbolic Interaction*. Chicago: University of Chicago Press, 1976.

———. *Portrait of American Jews: The Last Half of the 20th Century*. Seattle: University of Washington Press, 1995.

Henry, Bonnie. "Pioneer Synagogue: Old Temple to be Jewish Cultural Center." *Arizona Daily Star* (Sept. 14, 1994).

"Historic Addition to a 60's Temple." *Architecture* (May 1984), 208–11.

Holisher, Desider. *The House of God*. New York: Crown, 1946.

———. *The Synagogue and Its People*. New York: Abelard-Schuman, 1955.

Israelowitz, Oscar. *Synagogues of New York City*. New York: Dover Publications, 1982.

———. *Synagogues of the United States: A Photographic and Architectural Survey*. New York: Israelowitz Publishing, 1992.

Isaacs, A.S. "Recent American Synagogue Architecture." *American Architect and Building News* 94 (Sept. 2, 1908), 73–76.

Jacobus, John, Jr. *Philip Johnson.* Makers of Contemporary Architecture series. New York: Braziller, 1962.

Jick, Leon A. *The Americanization of the Synagogue: 1820–1870*. Hanover, N.H.: Brandeis University Press, 1976.

Kaufman, David. *Shul with a Pool: The "Synagogue-Center" in American Jewish History.* Brandeis Series in American Jewish History, Culture and Life. Hanover, N.H.: Brandeis University Press, 1998.

Kay, Jane Holtz. "Synagogue Architecture." *Midstream* XXIV:8 (1978), 43–49.

Kayser, Stephen S. "Visual Arts in American Jewish Life." *Judaism: A Quarterly Journal,* 3:4, 437–45.

Kline, Alexander, ed. *Contemporary Development in American Synagogue Art. CCAR Journal of the Union of American Hebrew Congregation* (Oct. 1956).

Kline, Alexander. "Synagogue Architecture in America." *The Reconstructionist* 18:10 (June 1952), 21–28.

Kramer, William M., and Reva Clar. "Rabbi Edgar F. Magnin and the Modernization of Los Angeles Jewry. Part 1." *Western States Jewish History* 19:3 (1987), 233–51.

Krinsky, Carol Herselle. *Synagogues of Europe*. Cambridge, Mass.: MIT Press, 1985.

———. "Gates of the Grove Synagogue: A New Space Encloses the Past, Present and Future." *Journal of the Interfaith Forum on Religion, Art & Architecture* (Winter 1989–90), 45–47.

———. "Judaism by Design." *Hadassah Magazine* (Nov. 1992), 46–49.

Kubany, Elizabeth. "Temple Beth Shalom." *Architectural Record* (July 1998), 88–91.

Lane, George, A. *Chicago Churches and Synagogues: An Architectural Pilgrimage*. Chicago: Loyola University Press, 1981.

"The Last Work of a Great Architect." *Architectural Forum* 102 (Feb. 1955), 106–15.

Levy, D.S. "Religious Relics." *Metropolis* (Apr. 1989), 84–92.

Levy, F.N. "Arnold Brunner." *American Magazine of Art* XVI (May 1925), 253ff.

Meier, Richard. *Recent American Synagogue Architecture*. New York: The Jewish Museum, 1963.

Mendelsohn, Eric. *Letters of an Architect*, ed. Oskar Beyer. London: Abelard-Schuman, 1967.

Moore, Deborah Dash. *To the Golden Cities: Pursuing the American Jewish Dream in Miami and L.A.* New York: Free Press, 1994.

Morganthaler, Hans R. "'It will be hard for us to find a home': Projects in the United States 1941–1953." In *Eric Mendelsohn Architect 1887–1953*, ed. Regina Stephan. New York: Monacelli Press, 1999.

Neusner, Jacob. *Understanding American Judaism, Volume One: The Rabbi and the Synagogue*. New York: Ktav Pub. House, 1975.

"North Shore Temple Israel." *Architecture International* 1 (1965), 96–103.

"Oheb Shalom." *Architectural Record* 135 (June 1964), 147–52.

Olitzky, Kerry M. "Synagogue: A New Concept for a New Age." *Journal of Jewish Communal Service* 62:1 (1985), 8–10.

———. *The American Synagogue: A Historical Dictionary and Sourcebook.* Westport, CT: Greenwood Press, 1996.

———. *An Encyclopedia of American Synagogue Ritual.* Westport, CT: Greenwood Press, 2000.

Pool, David de Sola, and Tamar Pool. *An Old Faith in the New World: Portrait of Shearith Israel, 1654–1954*. New York: Columbia University Press, 1955.

*Proceedings. Second National Conference and Exhibit on Synagogue Architecture and Art*. New York, Nov.-Dec. 1957.

Pruce, Earl. *Synagogues, Temples, and Congregations of Maryland: 1830–1990*. Baltimore: Jewish Historical Society of Maryland, 1993.

Rader, Lauren Weingarden. "Synagogue Architecture in Illinois." In *Faith and Form: Synagogue Architecture in Illinois. An Exhibiton Organized by the Spertus Museum*. Chicago: Spertus College Press, 1976.

Ransom, David F. "One Hundred Years of Jewish Congregations in Connecticut, An Architectural Survey: 1843–1943." *Connecticut Jewish History* 2:1 (1992), 7–147.

*Religious Buildings/by the editors of Architectural Record.* New York, Architectural Record, 1979.

"Rodeph Shalom Synagogue, Pittsburgh, Pennsylvania." *American Architect and Building News* 93: 1882 (Mar. 18, 1908), 97.

Rosenfeld, Erika. "The New Intimate Sanctuary." *Reform Judaism* (Fall, 1994),??.

Rovner, Ruth. "The Old and New in Atlanta." *New York Jewish Week* (June 11–17, 1993), 16–17.

Rudolph, B.G. *From a Minyan to a Community: A History of the Jews of Syracuse*. Syracuse, N.Y.: Syracuse University Press, 1970.

Sarna, Jonathan D. "The Debate over Mixed Seating in the American Synagogue." In *The American Synagogue: A Sanctuary Transformed*, ed. Jack Wertheimer. New York: Cambridge University Press, 1987), 363–94.

Schack, William. "Modern Art in the Synagogue II: Artist, Architect, and Building Committee Collaborate." *Commentary* 21 (1956), 152–61.

———. "Synagogue Art Today: I, Something of a Renaissance." *Commentary* 20 (1955), 548–53.

Schappes, Morris U., ed. *A Documentary History of the Jews in the United States 1654–1875*. New York: Schocken Books, 1971.

Scharlach, Bernice. "San Francisco." *Hadassah Magazine* (Jan. 1993), 24–29.

Schless, Nancy Halverson. "Peter Harrison, The Touro Synagogue, and the Wren City Church." *Winterthur Portfolio* 8 (1973), 187–200.

Schulze, Franz. *Philip Johnson: Life and Work*. New York: A.A. Knopf, 1994

Segal, Brenda. "Designing Temples in Accord with Nature, and Judaism Past and Present." *Jewish Post* IV:21 (Dec. 26, 1991), 3.

Seligman, Raphael. "A Tribute to Werner Seligman: A Son's Fond Memories of His Dad." *Temple Birth Sholom* (Sept. 2, 1999), 1, 6.

Silverstein, Alan. *Alternatives to Assimilation: The Response of Reform Judaism to American Culture 1840–1930*. Hanover, N.H.: Brandeis University Press, 1994.

Stein, Clarence S. "The Problem of the Temple and Its Solution." *Architectural Forum* 52 (Feb. 1930), 155–211.

Stern, Eugene N. "The Structural Frame of the New Temple Emanu-El building." *Architectural Forum* 49 (July 1928), 111–16.

Sussman, Lance J. "The Suburbanization of American Judaism as Reflected in Synagogue Building and Architecture, 1945–1975." *American Jewish History* 75 (Sept. 1985), 31–47.

"Synagogue." *Progressive Architecture* (Aug. 1954), 81, 89.

"Synagogue at Port Chester, U.S.A." *Architect and Building News* 218 (Dec. 28, 1960), 821–22.

"A Synagogue by Yamasaki." *Architectural Record* 135 (Sept. 1964), 191–96.

"Synagogue Design: Forcing an Aesthetic Unbound by Tradition." *P/A* (Mar. 1966), 146–50.

Tachau, William. "The Architecture of the Synagogue." *American Jewish Year Book* 28 (1926), 155–92.

"Temple Beth Israel." *Progressive Architecture* (Mar. 1952), 69–71.

"Temple Beth Zion, Buffalo, New York." *Inland Architect and News Record* 17:l (Feb. 1891).

"Temple Emanu-El, New York City." *Architecture and Building* 61 (Oct. 1929), 297–301.

"Temple's Slanting Walls Create an Upward Directed Symbolic Form." *Architectural Record* 143 (Mar. 1968), 133–136.

Tinterow, Gary. "Post World War II Synagogue Architecture." In *Two Hundred Years of American Synagogue Architecture*. Waltham, Mass.: Brandeis University, The Rose Art Museum, 1976), 30–34.

Treister, Kenneth. *Chapel of Light: Jewish Ceremonial Art in the Sophie & Nathan Gumenick Chapel*. New York: Union of American Hebrew Congregations, 2000.

"Vigorous Art in the Temple." *Architectural Forum* 110 (May 1959), 140–45.

Waddell, Gene. "An Architectural History of Kahal Kadosh Beth Elohim, Charleston." *South Carolina Historical Magazine* 98:1 (Jan. 1997), 6–55.

Whittick, Arnold. *Erich Mendelsohn*. New York: Dodge, 1956.

Wischnitzer, Rachel. *Synagogue Architecture in the United States: History and Interpretation*. Philadelphia: Jewish Publication Society, 1955.

Wong, Janay Jadine. "Synagogue Art of the 1950s: A New Context for Abstraction." *Art Journal* (Winter 1994), 37–43.

Yamasaki, Minoru. *A Life in Architecture*. New York: Weatherhill, 1979.

"Yamasaki's North Shore Congregation Israel." *Architectural Record* 135 (Sept. 1964), 191–96.

**Websites**

Chicago Architects Oral History Project
http://www.artic.edu/aic/collections/dept_architecture

Congregation Emanu-El of the City of New York
http://www.emanuelnyc.org

K.A.M. Isaiah Israel Congregation
http://www.kamii.org

North Shore Congregation Israel
http://www.nsci.org

Park Synagogue, Cleveland, Ohio
http://parksyn.org

Temple Beth Shalom, Miami Beach, Florida
http://www.tbsmb.org

Temple Beth Zion, Buffalo, New York
http://www.webt.com/tbz/bz
http://www.nmajh.org/exhibitions/postcards/cards/29.htm

Temple B'Nai Jehudah, Kansas City, Kansas
http://www.bnaijehuda.org

Temple Israel of Greater Miami, Miami, Florida
http://www.templeisrael.net

Temple Kol Ami, Scottsdale, Arizona
http://www.templekolami.org

Temple Mount Sinai, El Paso
http://www.templemountsinai.com

Temple Oheb Shalom, Baltimore, Maryland
http://www.templeohebshalom.org

The Temple, Atlanta, Georgia
http://www.the-temple.org

# Glossary



Ark: Commonly used name for the *Aron HaKodesh*, the cabinet in which the Torah scrolls are kept in a synagogue.

Aron ha-Kodesh: Holy Ark (cabinet for keeping Torah scrolls).

Ashkenazi (Ashkenazic): Derived from the term *Ashkenaz*, a medieval Hebrew term for Germany, it signifies the Jewish cultural milieu including western, central, and eastern Europe, and the Jews who emigrated from these areas to new lands.

Bar mitzvah*:* The ceremony held when a boy is thirteen years old, marking his passage into adulthood for religious purposes.

Bat mitzvah: Like the Bar mitzvah, but for girls. Begun only in the 1920s by the Conservative movement, it is now the norm in Reform, Conservative, and Reconstructionist congregations where women are allowed to read from the Torah and fully participate in every aspect of synagogue worship. On this day, the Bat Mitzvah leads the congregation in the service and enters the congregation as an "equal" member.

*Bet-ha-Knesset:* Literal translation from Hebrew is house of gathering/assembly; a synagogue.

*Bet-ha-Midrash:* Literal translation from Hebrew is a house of study. It may also refer to a synagogue.

*Bimah:* Platform or table in a synagogue from which the Torah scroll are read. Now used to refer to the platform in the front of many synagogues on which the Ark is also situated, and on which the congregational leaders, rabbi, and cantor sit.

*Cantor* (chazan): The chanter and leader of prayer in a synagogue.

Congregation: An independent religious association, usually housed in a synagogue.

Decalogue (Tablets of the Law): An artistic representation of the stone tablets on which were inscribed the Ten Commandments given by God to Moses on Mount Sinai.

Eternal Light (Hebrew: *Ner Tamid*): A continuously burning lamp that hangs before the Ark in a synagogue, meant to remind viewers of the omnipresence of God.

Five Books of Moses (*Pentateuch*): The first five books of the Hebrew Bible. These are the texts that are contained in the torah scrolls.

Gallery: An open upper story above an aisle of a nave. Traditionally, this space in the synagogue was reserved for women, though in Reform synagogues it was used for overflow seating.

Huppah: Canopy, usually of cloth, raised over the bride and groom at a Jewish wedding

Magen David: Star of David

Mechitzah: Divider separating mens' and womens' sections of synagogue

Menorah (pl. menorot*)*: A seven-branched candelabrum found in the biblical sanctuary and Jerusalem Temple; a similar candelabrum found in a synagogue; an eight-branched candelabrum used during the Hanukkah festival.

Mikvah (pl: mikvot): (Ritual bath) Facility employing fresh-flowing water, used for monthly cleansing ritual for women, and used for analogous rituals by men. Generally not used by Jews who follow Reform tendencies. Ritual baths were usually located near or even below the synagogue or community center.

Minyan: Ten adults (in orthodox practice, ten men) required for the reciting of prayers limited to community recitation.

Ner tamid: See Eternal Light.

Orthodox: Strictly adherent to traditional doctrine as embodied in the Torah, Talmud, and legal codes, as codified by sixteenth-century writers Joseph Caro and Moses Isserles.

Parochet: Curtain in front of Ark in a synagogue.

Rabbi: Traditionally a term of respect used for religious teachers, but now used for ordained Jewish ministers of religion.

Reader's Desk: Desk on which the Torah is placed for reading; in Hebrew *tevah* or *bimah*.

Reform Judaism: A movement that emerged in the early nineteenth century in Germany, and also in the United States, to simplify the Jewish liturgy and make it more accessible to a modern Jewish population. This included increased use of vernacular languages instead of Hebrew. The Reform movement in Germany tended to flourish among wealthier more assimilated Jews. In America, the movement that eventually coalesced into the Union of American Hebrew Congregations included members from all walks of life.

Responsa: The written opinions of rabbis in response to thorny questions of Jewish law and practice.

Sephardi (Sephardic): Referring to Jews and Jewish traditions originating in Spain and spreading throughout the world after the expulsion of the Jews from Spain in 1492. From the Hebrew *Sefarad* (Spain).

Shema: An essential prayer derived from the Torah (Deuteronomy 6:4–9) that has become the central creed of the Jewish people. It begins: "Hear, O Israel! The Lord is our God, the Lord is One." The prayer signifies the acceptance of the Torah and service to God.

*Shtetl*: Former small mostly Jewish towns of Eastern Europe.

*Sifrei Torah*: Torah scrolls.

Study House: Traditionally, a school and religious discussion room for Jewish male adults, often near or even attached to a synagogue. It may have an ark and a *bimah* so that people can use it for prayer. In America, in all but Orthodox synagogues, the study house has been replaced by religious school buildings geared to younger students.

Talmud: Record of legal decisions and discussions of ancient Jewish sages, the fundamental work of the Oral Law that complements the Written Law (Pentateuch). There are two versions of the Talmud: "Babylonia" and "Palestinian" or "Jerusalem." Each is divided into the Mishnah and the Gemara.

Temple: This refers to the main religious center of Jerusalem, the temple first built by King Solomon. Since the nineteenth century, the term "temple" has been increasing applied to synagogues, especially, but not exclusively, those of the Reform Movement.

Torah: Written Law, the Pentateuch (Five Books of Moses). Handwritten on parchment scrolls, it is kept in the synagogue Ark. The term is also used to describe all the writing of the bible and the commentaries (Written and Oral law).